PARENTING TEENS

PARENTING TEENS

Copyright © 2018 Dr. Stem Sithembile Mahlatini.
All rights reserved.
ISBN-978-1-7328275-0-9

All rights reserved. No part of this publication may be reproduced, stored in a retrieval system, or transmitted in any way by any means – electronic, mechanical, photocopy, recording, or otherwise – without the prior permissions of the copyright holder, except by reviewer who may quote brief passages in a review to be printed in magazine newspaper or by radio / TV announcement, as provided by USA copyright law. The author and the publisher will not be held responsible for any errors within the manuscript.

All characters appearing in this work are fictitious. Any resemblance to real persons, living or dead is purely coincidental.

Written by: Dr. Stem Sithembile Mahlatini Drstem14@gmail.com | www.drstemspeaks.com https://www.drstemmie.com/

Facebook: DrStem Mahlatini Twitter: DrStemahlatini LinkedIn: Drstem Mahlatini Skype: Dr.Mahlatini

Foreword by: Dr.Stem Sithembile Mahlatini Cover Design by: Masimba Mukundinashe

Photo: EdPedi Photography Studio & Gardens
www.edpediphoto.com

Category: Historical, Biographical, Motivational, Inspirational, Educational and Empowerment

Library of Congress Cataloging-in-Publication Data
Printed in the USA

Parenting Teens

FOREWORD

To every parent, the teenage years bring entirely new and alien creatures at times, and angels at other times. My hope with this guide is for you to find a medium that allows you to enjoy all of your teen's moments. I am sure you get so exhausted hearing things like "I'm bored", "you just don't understand", "why are you freaking out?", "I hate my life!", and so on. Be encouraged because your teenagers' years can be an amazing season of cultivating creativity, self-awareness, and passion for the things that really matter. The secret is in how you view this period that we will call the "Fight" Period' or "The Tough Times Period". This fight you are in right now, your teenager needs it.

Whaaaat? I know weird but they do benefit from the fights. As part of growing up and becoming self-sufficient, your teenager needs the disagreements and the annoyance to grow and learn.

If your teenager had the right words to explain this phase of their growth, they could say to you: "I need to hate you right now and I need you to survive it. I need you to survive my hating you and you hating me. I need this fight

even though I hate it too. It doesn't matter what this fight is even about: curfew, homework, laundry, messy room, going out, staying in, leaving, not leaving, boyfriend, girlfriend, no friends, bad friends. It doesn't matter. I need to fight you on it and I need you to fight me back.

I desperately need you to hold the other end of the rope. To hang on tightly while, yes, I do crazy stuff, say crazy stuff, take unnecessary risks—while I find the handholds and footholds in this new world I feel like I am in. I used to know who I was, who you were, who we were. But right now, I don't. Right now, I am looking for my limits and I can sometimes only find them when I am pulling on you. I know you long for the sweeter kid that I was. I know this because I long for that kid, too, and some of that longing is what is so painful for me right now because I must continue growing and fight through these teenage years.

I need this fight and I need to see that no matter how bad or big my feelings are, they won't destroy you or me. I need you to love me even at my worst, even when it looks like I don't love you. I need you to love yourself and me for the both of us right now.

I know it sucks to be disliked and labeled the bad guy. I feel the same way on the inside, but I need you to tolerate it and get other grownups to help you because I can't right now. No matter how bad things are between us or in our life, I depend on you, I really do. Please don't give up on me. I am a work in progress and there is nothing that would make me more happy than to make sure you are proud of me and happy with me and my life.

The difficult times between us teaches me that whatever I do to remember the good will always outweigh the bad. I need to focus on doing good. These fights teach me that bad feelings don't mean the end of a relationship, so let's not use words that hurt us both deeper than is necessary. We can have disagreements and still agree to disagree with respect for each other. This too will be a fight for us to reason and listen to each other.

Please remember the teenage years will end. Like any storm, it will blow over, and we will both forget. When the storm returns, I will need you to hang on to the rope again and be there for me, no matter what. I will need this over and over for years. No matter how distant I appear, I respect and love you, and you will always be my number one guide and guardian.

I hope this book gives you the guidance and answers that will help you tackle the big worries that keep most parents of teenagers awake at night.

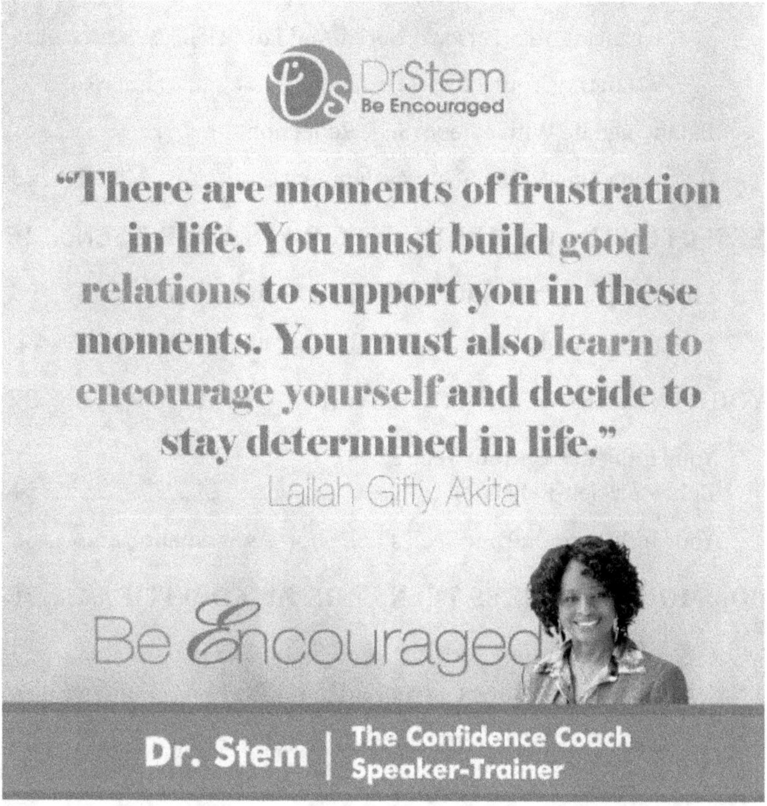

Dr. Stem—Be Encouraged

> "There are moments of frustration in life. You must build good relations to support you in these moments. You must also learn to encourage yourself and decide to stay determined in life."
> — Lailah Gifty Akita

Contents

SO, YOU'RE PARENTING A TEENAGER 11

BALANCING LIFE WITH A TEEN 13

Tips For Balancing Life And Your Teen 14
- Keeping An Eye Out On Your Teen While At Work 14
- Balancing Your Personal, Social And Love Life 15
- Balancing Your Love Life 17

Balancing Life With A Teen: Self-Reflection 21
Balancing Life With A Teen: Assignment 23

EFFECTIVELY COMMUNICATING WITH YOUR TEEN 25

Effectively Communicating With Your Teen: Self-Reflection 28
Effectively Communicating With Your Teen: Assignment 30

YOUR INFLUENCE ON YOUR TEEN'S BEHAVIOR 32

Your Influence On Your Teen's Behavior: Self-Reflection 34
Your Influence On Your Teen's Behavior: Assignment 36

COMMON PRESSURES TEENS ARE FACED WITH 38

- Understanding Identity 38
- Peer Pressure And Social Acceptance 40
- Drugs 40
- Alcohol 43
- Teenage Sex 44
- Sexually Transmitted Diseases (Stds) 47
- Teenage Pregnancy 48
- Sexting 49
- Bullying 50

Common Pressures Teens Are Faced With: Self-Reflection 53
Common Pressures Teens Are Faced With: Assignment 55

GETTING TO KNOW YOUR TEEN'S FRIENDS 57

Getting To Know Your Teen's Friends: Self-Reflection 59
Getting To Know Your Teen's Friends: Assignment 61

SUPPORTING YOUR TEEN'S EMOTIONS 63

Depression And Suicide 63
Stress And Anxiety 65
Supporting Your Teen's Emotions? Self- Reflection 66
Supporting Your Teen's Emotions: Assignment 68

LOVE, DATING AND RELATIONSHIPS 70

Dating: The Point Of It All 70
How Do I Know When My Teen Is Ready To Date? 71
How Do I Explain Love To My Teen? 73
What If My Teen Experiences Heartbreak? 75
What If My Teen Is Unsure About Their Sexual Orientation? 76
Love, Dating And Relationships: Self- Reflection 78
Love, Dating And Love, Dating And Relationships: Assignment 80

SUPPORTING YOUR TEEN'S GOALS 82

What Is A Personal Goal? 82
Tips For Helping Your Teen Achieve Their Goals 84
Supporting A College Bound Teen 85
Preparing Your Teen For College 86
What If My Teen Is Not Interested In College? 88
Supporting Your Teen's Personal Goals: Self-Reflection 89
Supporting Your Teen's Personal Goals: Assignment 91

RAISING TEEN GIRLS 93

Physical Appearance 93
    Dieting 94
Self-Image 95
    Menstrual Cycles 95
Tips To Help Your Teen Girl Embrace Her Changing Body 97

RAISING TEEN BOYS 99

Physical Appearance 99
Sex And Hormones 100
Masculinity, Self-Image And Social Expectations 100
    Benefits For Your Children 107
    Separating Feelings From Behavior 108
    Don't Put Your Children In The Middle 109
    Improving Communication With Your Co-Parent 110
    Co-Parenting Communication Methods 111
    Aim For Co-Parenting Consistency 113
    Making Important Decisions As Co-Parents 114
    Resolving Co-Parenting Disagreements 115
    When Your Child Leaves 116
    When Your Child Returns 117
    Dealing With Visitation Refusal 118
Affirmational Thoughts And Next Steps 119
Let's Connect 121
About The Author 122
Training, Individual And Group Life Coaching 126

BONUS 130

Text Message Codes Used By Teenagers Today 130

So, You're Parenting a Teenager

Congratulations! You've successfully raised your child to be a healthy, thriving teenager. Long gone are the days of changing diapers, changing soiled outfits, mixing bottles, reading bedtime stories, and playing with Legos and baby dolls. Your teen is now ready for self-exploration and exploring the world around them.

You might be thinking to yourself, "I'm not ready for this phase—bring back the bedtime stories". It's perfectly normal to miss the days when your teen was a child. In fact, you might feel that they've grown way too fast. Maybe you feel like you lost time with them during their childhood and want to rekindle that time.

The teenage years are a great time to establish a meaningful relationship. It won't always be easy. You might even encounter times when you're not sure you know who your teen is anymore. However, there will certainly be several opportunities for you to share your wisdom and bond with your teen if done right. Keeping an open line of communication and allowing yourself to grow along with your teen is important.

Perhaps you feel the relationship you have with your teen is just perfect and you want to make sure your relationship remains strong. That's great! We'll discuss all the things you need to know to support your teen so that they're well equipped for adulthood. We'll also provide suggestions for nurturing your relationship along the way.

Parents are the ultimate role models for children. Every word, movement and action has an effect. No other person or outside force has a greater influence on a child than the parent.
– Bob Keeshan

If you want your teenagers to turn out well, trust and believe them more than they believe in themselves. **–DrStem**

Balancing Life with a Teen

Balancing your life and the life of a teen can get complicated. You might have already noticed that your teenager's schedule has required you to alter your own. Your teen might be involved in extracurricular activities that require a lot more of your time. Their social life might have you feeling like a personal chauffeur because they're always "on the go" with friends. Perhaps they even have a part- time job.

So, how do you balance it all, especially since you have your own life to balance? You have a job and social life of your own. Whether you work in the home or travel outside of the home for employment, your job requires your time and focus. Your social life is also necessary so that you continue to feel connected with others, some of which might also be parents of teens.

Not to mention, your love life needs to remain intact. Whether you're married or a single parent on the dating scene, it takes time to establish and maintain a relationship. You might find it difficult to do this while raising a teen.

Most importantly, you need "me" time—time to take care of yourself. This concept might be a little hard for some parents, but it's important to take care of yourself so that you're healthy enough and of a sound mind to effectively support your teen.

Tips for Balancing Life and Your Teen

There are several things you can do to balance your personal life without feeling as though you're neglecting your teen or burning yourself out. Let's explore them.

Keeping an Eye Out on Your Teen While at Work

It's normal to worry about what your teen might be up to while they're home alone after school or during the weekend alone. This is a genuine concern since several studies suggest that teens tend to engage in risky behavior between the hours of 3 pm and 6 pm, which happens to be when most parents are away from home. One way to address this is by providing your teen with a cell phone so that you have a way to keep in touch with them when you're away. If you're not comfortable with your teen having a phone, consider a basic phone with limited contacts and features. Your cell phone carrier can also recommend apps for limiting and monitoring cellular activity.

You might also consider enrolling your teen in an after-school program or extracurricular activity after school and on the weekends.

Search for programs in your area that align with your teen's interests and get them involved. Many community-based programs are free or low cost. This helps to keep your teen occupied when you're away and can even enhance their learning experience since many after-school programs include homework assistance and tutoring.

Consider mentors who can help keep an eye on your teen. This can be a neighbor, teacher, coach, grandparent, uncle, aunt or church member. The phrase, "It takes a village to raise a child" might sound cliché, but it's very true. Mentors are responsible individuals who you trust and can also establish a meaningful relationship with your teen that allows them to effectively provide guidance and advice.

Even if their schedules don't allow them to keep constant watch over your teen, it's still beneficial to be able to call upon a mentor for emergencies or engage them in important conversations with your teen that you might struggle with addressing on your own. Mentors are not meant to replace you as a parent.

However, they can provide you with additional support.

BALANCING YOUR PERSONAL, SOCIAL AND LOVE LIFE

It is important that you are present in every aspect of your teen's life. However, you can easily stretch yourself too thin while attempting to accommodate your teens changing needs. Be sure to take care of yourself so that you are of sound mind and in good health to support your teen. If you fail to do this, you can allow stress to put your peace of mind and health at risk. Stress isn't just a feeling of frustration; it can also lead to a weakened immune system, heart disease and other chronic diseases.

Dealing with conditions such as these can make it even more difficult to balance life with your teen.

Find things you love to do—your favorite hobby, reading a book, watching your favorite television show, soaking in a long bath, and commit to doing at least one of them once or twice a week. Take time to destress so that when stressful circumstances concerning your teen present themselves, you have room to process them and respond effectively. Make sure you commit to spending this time with yourself. Help your teen to understand that taking "me time" is not a selfish act, it is essential so that you are your best self for them.

Finding balance also requires social support. This might mean spending time with friends, being active in a parent group, a faith- based organization or even volunteering in the community. We all need social connection to remind ourselves that we're human. Socializing allows us to feel connected; it's how we receive advice, inspiration, confirmation, personal and professional support, and exchange resources. You might be more or less inclined to engage socially, depending on your personality, but it's important to have someone or some group to reach out to for support.

Scheduling is critical to maintaining a healthy balance. These days, you aren't the only one with a social life because your teen has one, too. Balancing both can sometimes seem next to impossible. Take some time with your teen to distinguish nonpriority activities from those that are of high priority and establish how often activities that are nonpriority should take place. This will allow you to create a schedule and establish boundaries with regard to your time.

For example, you might agree to drive your teen to football or band practice as often as required but limit driving them to the mall or movies to once a week. If your teen is driving, this is an opportunity to share responsibility for getting to and from certain places during the week. Like you, teens need social connection, but it's up to you to determine how much and with who.

Scheduling also allows you to compare your teen's activities to your work schedule in advance so that you can change shifts or arrange for time off ahead of time, if necessary. Planning in advance will save you a ton of stress and disappointment from your teen.

Balancing Your Love Life

Whether you're married or single and dating, parenting a teen can impact the amount of time and energy you have to be physically and emotionally intimate. However, maintaining your relationship with your spouse or significant other is just as important as taking care of yourself.

If you're married, you and your spouse might notice that you're always "on the go", leaving little room for you to connect. In some cases, spouses find themselves disagreeing about how to parent their teen, causing a strain on their relationship. This is why it's important to take time to talk with your spouse about the type of support you need from them as a spouse and a parent.

It's important to make clear to your spouse what your concerns and goals are so that you can support one another where needed. Schedule time alone at least once or twice a week to talk about your parenting goals and check in with one another about your progress. Likewise, schedule time to connect as a married couple so that the relationship between the two of you remains strong. Make a conscious effort to separate conversations about your teen from intimate conversations between the two of you. Remember, your teen is an extension of your love for one another.

Maintaining a strong relationship will also strengthen your ability to parent together.

If you're single and dating, don't be afraid to share this with your teen. Many parents are concerned about when is the best time to introduce the person they're dating to their teen. Once you've established that the person you're dating is someone you can trust, the most important thing is that you explain to your teen why you're dating so that they're not confused about the process or feel that it will change your relationship with them.

Explain to your teen that you're interested in a life partner and need to make time to get to know other people who might be the right fit. Make clear that you dating doesn't mean you will love them any less. It's also important to make clear that you dating does not mean you respect their biological parent any less. It simply means that you want to share your love with someone else long-term and you're being diligent about determining who that person might be.

You can set an excellent example for what dating should look like for your teen by dating responsibly. This means demonstrating that you're dating with an end goal in mind—finding someone who shares your interests, can support your dreams, and loves you for who you are.

Be careful not to give your teen the impression that dating is all about fun and sex by openly exposing them to multiple sexual partners. It's also important not to change who you are, personality or otherwise, during the dating phase of your life. Remember, your teen is listening to and watching everything that you do and will likely model your behavior.

If you're not dating, continue to focus on you— your dreams, your goals, your well-being.

Living your best life will ultimately have a positive impact on your teen.

To be in your children's memories tomorrow, you have to be present in their lives today.
–Unknown

ch love never spoils children. Children spoiled when we substitute "presents"

" for "Presence". –*Anthony Witham* "

Balancing Life with a Teen: Self-Reflection

- What are you currently struggling to balance most with your teen? What can you do to improve your balance?

- What things do you enjoy doing the most? Which of these things can you commit to doing once or twice a week?

- If you're married or co-parenting, what type of support do you need from your partner to parent more effectively?

- If you're dating, what are at least three things you require before introducing them to your teen? What concerns you most about dating with a teen?

_____
_____
_____
_____
_____
_____
_____
_____
_____
_____

Balancing Life with a Teen: Assignment

△ Create a list of all your teen's activities, including socializing with their friends. Then, mark whether or not each activity on the list is of high priority. Discuss how often those activities that are not marked high priority should take place and develop a schedule.

Once the schedule is finalized, place it somewhere visible for you both to see.

_____
_____
_____
_____
_____
_____
_____
_____
_____
_____
_____
_____
_____
_____

EFFECTIVELY COMMUNICATING WITH YOUR TEEN

The teenage years require lots of communication. But, before you can begin to address any topics of concern with your teen, you must understand how to communicate with them effectively. Otherwise, what you think you're sharing out of love and concern might easily be misconstrued as being harsh or judgmental. It's important to enter into every conversation with an intent to share, understand and find resolve. If you enter into a conversation with your teen without being intentional about the outcome, it won't have much meaning in the long run. In fact, it might only leave you and your teen more frustrated than before you began the discussion.

Here are a few tips for communicating with your teen effectively:

- Share why you're asking certain questions or interested in discussing certain topics.
- Welcome your teen's insight on what they think or how they feel.
- Set rules for what is acceptable and what's not when communicating with one another. Though you want

their feedback, it's important to set clear boundaries on how you communicate with one another and establish respect. For example, no yelling, storming off, rolling eyes or using cellphones during conversation.

- Be transparent. If your teen asks a question, don't shy away from answering. What you don't share with them, they'll seek somewhere else. You're much more informative than their peers!

- If the conversation gets awkward or uncomfortable, acknowledge this, but don't use it as an excuse to cease communication. Likewise, if a conversation becomes heated and you're both angry or frustrated, acknowledge this. Put the conversation on hold and revisit it once you're both calm.

- Empathize with your teen when having discussions with them, good or bad. Teens need to feel that they're being understood.

- Affirm what your teen is saying to you through active communication. Repeat what you think they're saying to you and ask if you're understanding correctly. This sends a signal to your teen that you're actively listening and engaged in what they're saying.

Remember that your teen will often respond based on your approach and response. The wrong approach or response could potentially make what would have been a great conversation into one that is completely unproductive. It could also heighten an already tense conversation even more.

Miscommunication can leave your teen feeling misunderstood and damage their self-esteem. Communicate often so they know they're heard and that you care.

Effectively Communicating with Your Teen: Self-Reflection

△ Think of a difficult conversation you've had with your teen. How did you approach the conversation? What was the result? Is there anything you could have done better?

△ Think of a conversation you need to have with your teen that you've not yet had. What concerns you most about having this discussion? How can you approach the discussion?

_____
_____
_____
_____
_____
_____
_____
_____
_____
_____
_____

Effectively Communicating with Your Teen: Assignment

△ Make time to have the discussion that you previously described as part of the self- reflection exercise with your teen. Use the tips for effectively communicating with your teen to help guide you. Write down the outcome of the conversation and the tips that helped you most once the conversation is over.

_____

_____

_____

_____

_____

_____

_____

_____

_____

_____

_____

_____

_____

Your Influence on Your Teen's Behavior

The nonverbal cues you send to your teen are just as important as your verbal communication. Because teens are sorting out who they are and what their place is in the word, they observe and absorb everything.

Needless to say, what you do influences their behavior. This includes the way you talk, what you talk about, how your groom/dress, your work ethic, your recreational activity, how you address life's challenges, and how you deal with your emotions.

You can control what your teen absorbs at home. It goes without saying that what your teen observes in the home influences how they behave outside of the home. For example, if a teen is accustomed to hearing yelling in the home when emotions run high, they are more likely to yell when upset in other settings.

Likewise, if your teen observes smoking or drinking in the home, they are likely to engage in this behavior outside of the home. They're also paying attention to how you treat people and handle relationships. Even if you talk to your teen about not engaging in negative behaviors, it will likely "go into one ear and out of the other" if your actions give them the impression that it's not a big deal.

It is important to consistently model positive behavior. This includes your attitude about life. Maintaining a positive attitude and keeping your composure when times get tough can demonstrate to your teen that they can handle any situation in a constructive manner. Your lifestyle is also greatly influential. The way you dress, the foods you eat, and even the types of information you consume through the television can all influence your teen's perception of themselves, their overall health and their interests.

Parents often don't realize just how much their actions influence their teens because it seems their teen isn't very interested in what they have to say. This is especially true since many teens tend to have less interest in spending time with their parents during this phase of self- exploration. However, teens often times pay more attention to nonverbal cues than they do verbal cues. For example, you might tell your teen to clean their room until you're blue in the face, but if you take their cell phone away or take away their privilege to attend an event with their friends, you have their attention. Say what you mean, mean what you say, and behave in a way that you would want your teen to behave. Remember, you're preparing your teen for adulthood, so never take the impact of your actions on your teen lightly.

Your Influence on Your Teen's Behavior: Self-Reflection

△ What are some things you observed growing up in your home that still influence your behavior or perspective on life?

△ What are some things you do that you think positively influence your teen's behavior? What are some things you do that you think negatively influence your behavior? How can you change this?

_____
_____
_____
_____
_____
_____
_____
_____
_____
_____
_____

Your Influence on Your Teen's Behavior: Assignment

△ Talk to your teen about things they see you do or hear you say that make them feel positive and safe. Ask them if there's anything you do or say that makes them feel unsafe or negative in any way. Make a list of the things your teen shares with you. Continue to do those things that have a great influence on your teen and identify ways to change behaviors that negatively impact your teen.

_____
_____
_____
_____
_____
_____
_____
_____
_____
_____
_____
_____

Common Pressures Teens Are Faced With

Your teen is going through many physical and emotional changes due to hormones that we'll explore in more detail later on. In addition to the personal changes they're experiencing, they are faced with making sense of the changing world around them in the midst of constant pressure. This isn't easy, considering the fact that their brains are not yet fully mature.

Understanding Identity

The teenage years is a critical time for establishing identity. One of the things that contributes to your teen's actions and how they respond to the world around them is their understanding of who they are. They are constantly surrounded by people and circumstances that influence their perception of themselves and ultimately, their behavior.

Personality plays a part in your teen's identity. By nature, your teen might be an introvert, which means they are less likely to want to choose socializing over staying to themselves. For example, an introverted teen might enjoy their own company by reading a book or listening to music. On the other hand, an extroverted teen is more likely to be interested in being surrounded by others.

These are what we call "social butterflies". Some teens easily adapt between the two.

Your teen's environment is a major factor in how your teen sees their identity. The way you raise your teen, what they observe emotionally and physically, and their family culture can all contribute to how your teen identifies with themselves. For example, a teen raised in a home where freedom of speech is welcome might identify themselves as being more liberal than a teen who is raised in a home where sharing their opinions is restricted.

Similarly, a teen girl whose mother is a homemaker or helps to raise several younger siblings might identify herself as being a caregiver, whether at home or in the workplace. A teen boy might identify himself as a provider if his father is a diligent worker or his mother demands that he help out around the house (i.e., taking out the trash, cutting the grass, working a part-time job).

Traumatic experiences can cause teens to struggle with their identity. Examples of this might include, divorce, witnessing verbal or physical abuse, enduring physical or emotional abuse, or death in the family. These types of experiences can lead to self-doubt, lack of trust, low self-esteem or feeling unsure about who they are. Likewise, positive experiences in the home can impact the way your teen sees themselves. For example, reminding your teen of how strong, smart, beautiful and loved they are can result in a strong self-esteem. Paying attention to and constantly pointing out their strengths also helps their self-esteem.

Peer Pressure and Social Acceptance

Your teen will be faced with circumstances outside of the home that will inevitably influence their behavior. Perhaps the most dangerous type of pressure your teen will be face is being socially accepted. Everything seems to be trending—even things your teen might not be comfortable with, but that doesn't stop their peers from trying to convince them to "try it", nor does it stop their natural inclination to want to fit in. This is what we call peer pressure.

Peer pressure is an influence from a person or group to conform to their expectations.

Your teen might experience peer pressure at school, from close friends, family members or even distant strangers on social media.

For a teen, being accepted by their peers makes them feel special and gives them a sense of validation. Teens with low self-esteem are especially influenced by peer pressure because being accepted gives them a sense of belonging. Unfortunately, falling victim to peer pressure in an effort to feel liked or accepted can lead teens to a dangerous path. For example, many teens boys fall victim to gangs because of their desire to belong. It is also common for teenage girls to fall victim to teenage pregnancy due to their desire to be loved.

Drugs

Recreational drugs are everywhere. Many teens participate in drug use because it seems like something fun to do. Some do it because they want people around them to think they're cool or to try to fit in. Others do it because they think it will help them take away their emotional or physical pain. Either way, using drugs makes teens more susceptible to drug addiction.

Taking drugs will not eliminate emotional pain. Drugs might temporarily distract a person from their pain, but this fleeting distraction leads them to depend on the drug over and over again, which leads to drug dependence— also known as drug addiction. This means, eventually, their bodies begin to depend on the drug to the point where they can't function without it. Drug use can inhibit normal brain function and prevent the ability to make rational decisions. This can be devastating to a teen since they're still developing. Drug dependency can consume your teen's entire life, causing them to lose their focus and their sense of self.

Drugs impact circuits in the brain. They especially affect what's called the limbic system by causing dangerously large amounts of dopamine to flood a teen's system. This causes a shift in the way their brain functions and can prevent them from thinking clearly.

Drug use can also lead to lung and heart disease overtime. Some drugs are made of deadly chemicals that can send your teen into a coma or cause their heart to stop immediately upon taking them.

There's no such thing as a safe drug. One of the most common traps that teens fall into is believing that a drug isn't harmful because of its trendy name, or that one drug is less harmful than another. The fact is, all drugs are dangerous, no matter the type or how large or small the amount. Even smoking cigarettes is a gateway to other drugs because it introduces your teen's body to nicotine and leads to dependency.

It's important to talk to your teen about restraining form taking any type of substance, no matter how harmless it might seem. These days, drugs aren't called "drugs" anymore.

They have fun, trendy names that make them appear harmless. Most teens don't know what they're actually consuming when they take what they think is a "harmless drug". For example, marijuana, which has negative effects of its own, can have even worse effects if laced with other lethal drugs, such as cocaine. Drugs don't come with instructions, ingredients or warning labels. There's simply no way of knowing what your teen might actually be putting into their body.

Prescription drugs are no exception. Another dangerous misconception is that taking a prescription drugs is safer than taking drugs that aren't prescribed by a doctor. This is false! Even drugs prescribed by a doctor can be dangerous if the drug was not originally prescribed for the person consuming them, or if it's not taken according to the doctor's orders.

For example, teens are increasingly overdosing on opioids (pain pills) that has been prescribed to a family member or a friend.

Opioids are thought to "take the edge off" or numb pain since they are created as pain killers. However, improper dosage of these drugs can lead to immediate death.

Let your teen know that no matter how diligent their peers might be in convincing them that using certain drugs can take their mind off of things or help loosen them up for fun, it's not worth risking their life over.

Alcohol

Even if your teen has no intention of using drugs, their friends might try to convince them that alcohol is ok. Your teen might even observe close family members routinely drink alcohol as recreation. However, teenage drinking is not ok! In fact, alcohol can have many of the same negative effects on their brain as drugs.

Like drugs, many teens think that drinking alcohol makes them appear more mature or helps them to fit in. There's also a misconception that alcohol will enhance their ability to have fun. However, alcohol actually reduces the brain's ability to make sound decisions, which makes it harder for the conscious to kick in when it needs to.

Not being able to think clearly can be very dangerous! Your teen can easily find themselves somewhere unconscious or have a dangerous fall. They might also subject themselves to having someone take advantage of them or date rape. A large majority of teens who engage in sexual or criminal activity also engage in recreational drinking.

Abstaining from alcohol can prevent your teen from experiencing awful side effects caused by drinking, such as dizziness, nausea and vomiting. Your teen might even be able to save a life if they're in a situation where they're the only person among a group of friends who is not intoxicated.

Drinking alcohol can lead to addiction and poor health. This is considered a critical stage of development for what is required of the brain as an adult, such as critical thinking and decision-making. Teenage drinking can lead to brain damage which can cause memory loss or the loss of motor skills. Drinking can also lead to liver and other chronic diseases over time.

Teens who begin drinking before the age of 21 are more likely to develop alcohol addiction, which increases their chances of chronic illness and premature death.

Teenage Sex

Teenage sex is perhaps one of the biggest forms of peer pressure your teen might face. This is especially true if the peer is someone that your teen really likes. Teens will often describe sex as "not a big deal". That's because, these days, sex doesn't have much meaning to teens. It's considered to be more of an act of recreation. You might have even heard it referred to as recreational sex. It's about popularity, having fun, fitting in, and wanting to be accepted or loved.

According to the 2015 National Youth Risk Behavior Survey (YRBS) conducted by the Centers for Disease Control and Prevention (CDC), 41% of high school students have ever had intercourse and 30% of high school students are currently sexually active. Of the students who are currently sexually active, 21% drank alcohol or used drugs before their last sexual intercourse. Because teenage sex is so common, open lines of communication about sex and the circumstances that come with it is critically important.

Sex is more than a feeling. At this stage, every teenager wants to feel loved and accepted. The idea of someone wanting to be intimate with them might make them feel flattered and incredibly desirable. They might even feel butterflies or unusually excited. This might lead your teen to believe they have a physical or emotional connection, also referred to as "chemistry" with someone. However, what they're actually feeling is their hormones at work. This is why they should never make the decision to engage in sexual activity with anyone because of how they feel.

Sex is not just about fun and games. Many teens treat sex as a competitive sport. For example, who can sleep with who first, who can do it better or last the longest. Some teens even have sex out of jealousy because they want to keep the attention of a certain individual or prove to their peers that they're more popular.

The truth is, sex is not just a fun sport. It's a form of bonding that has long-lasting effects. Did you know that your brain actually releases a chemical called oxytocin when having sex, which is the same chemical released when mothers breastfeed their babies to help them bond? That's how powerful oxytocin is. So, the idea that a teen can just have sex for the fun of it is completely false! It's a lot more complicated than that.

Sex affects teens emotionally. It can be rather hard for a teen to emotionally distance themselves from someone they've had sex with. What they think might be fun or lead to love could actually leave them feeling rejected and empty in the long run. These feelings can ultimately harm their self-esteem.

Many times, teens engage in sex because there are trying to fill a void. For example, not having both parents in the home or being abused and neglected could all result in voids that make the idea of someone wanting to have sex with them seem appealing. Teens can have false hope that having sex will make them feel better about themselves if their self-esteem is low. Like drugs and alcohol, sex can be used to temporarily numb or distract them from pain. However, sex is only a temporary distraction from a larger problem. Sex can also be addictive.

Sex does not equal love. It is important to explain to your teen that, though people who love one another have sex when the time is right, the act of sex itself does not mean they're proving their love. Teenage hormones can often times cause teens to feel physically connected to someone at a very fast pace, which can easily be mistaken for love. Warn your teen not to fall for this trap.

Another trap that teens fall into is being convinced that they need to have sex to prove their love for someone. Explain to your teen that real love doesn't pressure anyone to do anything they're uncomfortable with doing. If someone truly loves them, they would not be pressured into having sex. The best time to introduce sex into a relationship is during a marriage, when they're committed to one person for a lifetime.

It is also important to tell your teen not to ever try to convince a person to have sex with them by telling them they love them. Doing this can have negative emotional effects on the other person long-term. Someone else's mental health is not worth their personal pleasure.

Sexually Transmitted Diseases (STDs)

Some teens believe they can keep their emotions under control by having "casual" sex. They believe that if they can manage to have sex without getting their emotions involved, it will prevent them from getting hurt. However, getting involved with multiple partners only increases their risk of being hurt, especially if they contract a sexually transmitted disease (STD).

STDs have long-term effects. The most common forms of STDs are chlamydia, gonorrhea, genital herpes, human papillomavirus (HPV), syphilis and HIV. Although chlamydia and gonorrhea are treatable, they aren't treated overnight, and they can have long-term effects later in adulthood. Both of these infections can cause unpleasant orders, discharges, and lots of itching and swelling. Over time, these infections can lead to cervical cancer in women or complications with becoming pregnant. It can also lead to sterilization in men. HIV and genital herpes are not curable. If your teen contracts these viruses, they will remain with them for a lifetime.

While sexually transmitted diseases (STDs) affect individuals of all ages, STDs take a particularly heavy toll on teens and young adults. The CDC estimates that youth ages 15-24 make up just over one quarter of the sexually active population, but account for half of the 20 million new sexually transmitted infections that occur in the United States each year. Teens tend to think they're invincible and that chances are, it won't happen to them.

However, these statistics show us just how common contracting a STD as a teen really is. Even more troubling, some STDs come with little to no symptoms, which makes them harder to detect and easier to spread.

No form of sexual activity or protection is 100% safe. Teens can easily be convinced that they're safe from these infections as long as they use protection (i.e., condoms). They might also believe that engaging in other forms of sex, such as oral sex, is safer. However, STDs are spread through the exchange of bodily fluid, and oral sex certainly does not exclude this type of exchange. Likewise, condoms are not 100% guaranteed to prevent leakage of bodily fluid.

Bodily fluid isn't the only thing to be concerned about. Genital herpes can be contracted simply through skin to skin contact—no fluid necessary. So, encourage your teen to think twice before deciding to engage in *any* type of sexual activity.

Teenage Pregnancy

Aside from contracting a STD, having sex can lead to an unplanned pregnancy. Having a baby as a teen comes with a great deal of responsibility and can lead to extremely high levels of stress. Teenage parents are responsible for supporting both themselves and their baby. This is extremely difficult considering they're still growing themselves.

Make clear to your teen that babies require lots of time, money and attention, which will require them to spend a lot less time, money and attention on the things they enjoy. It is also very common for teenage parents to struggle with finishing school. Teen mothers also commonly struggle with what's called post- partum depression, which is a type of depression that presents itself after a woman delivers her baby. Furthermore, supporting a baby at an early age can cause emotional distress for all parties involved.

If your teen thinks they might already be pregnant or impregnated someone else, seek help from a medical physician right away.

Pregnancy can affect your teen's emotions and health, and the health of the baby, so it's important to surround them with a strong support system. Though this can be a very difficult circumstance to work through, and might cause you great disappointment, your teen needs your love and support more than ever.

If you suspect that your teen is having sex or is pregnant but they're not talking to you, try having a conversation with them about their relationships and experiences with being a teenager so far without readily accusing or judging them. Ask questions that make it safe for them to open up to you and reiterate how much you care about them and want to support them through anything they're going through.

Sexting

Explain to your teen that sexting is never a good alternative to having sex. Sexting involves taking and sending explicit pictures or messages to someone. Teens might be convinced that sexting is ok because they're not actually engaging in the act. However, sexting is never ok. Not only does it entice the person who's receiving these texts and images to engage in sexual activity, it also jeopardizes the privacy of the person who sends the messages. Once a "sext" is in the hands of the person who received it, the content of the "sext" is subject to being shared with anyone, anywhere. This might mean that the messages are forwarded to other people's phones or even circulated on the internet!

Sending sexual images to minors is also against the law. Some states have even begun prosecuting minors for child pornography or felony obscenity. Tell your teen to make you aware if they ever receive a "sext" so that you can protect them.

Bullying

Teens are consistently faced with being bullied by their peers. The constant feeling of not being liked or being threatened can diminish a teen's sense of self-worth and even cause them to live in fear. Though the concept of bullying might seem cliché to teens because they often tease each other for fun, talk to your teen about how their peers make them feel.

Ask them if they've after felt devalued or threatened by anyone through social media or otherwise.

Social media is often used as a tool for cyber bullying. Unfortunately, many people use social media to embarrass, harass or threaten others. This is called cyber bullying. Cyber bullying can also happen over text messages or email. Your teen might not understand how it's possible to be bullied by someone who they can't see or hear. However, explain to them that reading negative words that target them on a consistent basis can cause them to internalize what is being said.

Threatening words can also cause anxiety and fear.

Cyber bullying can have harmful emotional effects. If your teen is affected by cyber bullying frequently or over a long period of time, they can develop anxiety, stress and even depression. In fact, teens who experience high incidences of cyber bullying also have higher incidences of suicidal thoughts or attempts.

Encourage your teen to make you aware if they experience threats or harassing comments by text or social media. Even if your teen isn't personally affected by the comments they receive, the person doing the bullying is likely bullying others who are being affected. Sadly, many teens don't speak up when they're being cyber bullied because they're afraid that sharing this information will embarrass them even more.

Bullying is not limited to social media. Bullying can happen at school, over the phone or anywhere. Explain to your teen that it's never ok for anyone to constantly harass them or make them feel uncomfortable in any way. Ask your teen to let you know if this is happening.

It's also important to talk to your teen about refraining from bullying others. If they are bullying anyone, put a stop to it right away! They might be bullying someone because they don't like the person or simply because everyone else is doing it. Regardless of how they might feel about a person, harassment is never ok. Even if they find themselves in a situation where their friends or classmates are bullying someone, tell them not to engage. This behavior is unnecessary and can be harmful.

Common Pressures Teens are Faced With: Self-Reflection

- What pressures did you deal with as a teen? How are they different from the pressures teens are experiencing today? What can you do to try to identify with the pressures your teen might be experiencing?

- If you were to discover that your teen has tried drugs or is drinking alcohol, how would you handle it? What can you do to prevent this type of behavior?

- Does your teen talk to you about sex? If so, what types of questions do they ask? How might you revisit these questions as follow-up? If not, what might you tell your teen to help them feel comfortable with talking to you about sex?

- Has your teen ever been bullied? How did this experience impact them? What might you tell your teen to help boost their self-esteem?

_____

_____

_____

_____

Common Pressures Teens are Faced With: Assignment

△ Make a list of all the pressures you were faced with as a teen. Take some time to share your list with your teen and ask them talk to you about anything they can relate to. Then, ask them if they are experiencing any pressures that you don't have listed. Ask questions about what they're experiencing and how you can support them.

_____
_____
_____
_____
_____
_____
_____
_____
_____
_____
_____
_____

Getting to Know Your Teen's Friends

Your teen's friends impact their decisions. Even if your teen has never engaged in any of the activities already described, they might have friends who are actively engaged in these activities. This might make engaging in unhealthy behavior more tempting.

As a parent, you have influence over who your teen spends time with while they're under your watch. This means monitoring who they invite over to the house, whose house they visit, who they talk to on the phone, and even who they're engaging with on social media.

So, how do you know whether or not your teen's friends are trustworthy and a good influence? You can usually sense this right away based on their conversation with one another. You can also pay attention to their behavior when their friends are around. Here are a few questions you can ask when assessing your teen's friends:

- Do your teen's friends come from a troubled household? If so, do they demonstrate any bad habits? Be careful not to judge a book by its cover. Just because a teen comes from a troubled home doesn't mean they're not trustworthy. Be sure to make your decision based on the teen's manners and actions.

- Are your teen's friends respectful?

- Is your teen's friends responsible?

- Do you know the parents of your teen's friends? If so, do you feel you can keep an open line of communication with them?

- Are your teen's friends a bad influence on your teen? Do you notice negative changes in behavior or mood when your teen is around any of their friends or immediately after having spent time with any of them?

- Do your teen's friends share the same values as your teen?

- Do your teen's friends help bring out the best in your teen?

You can also screen through your teen's social media accounts to observe the types of comments and pictures your teen's friends are sharing. These days, teens are "friending" people online that they've never even met. Be sure that the people your teen is engaging with online are not a negative influence. Encourage your teen to befriend people who bring out the best in them and care about their best interest. Establishing meaningful, supportive relationships now can follow them well into adulthood.

It's also important to explain to your teen that they should never agree to meet in person with anyone they meet online. This is especially dangerous for teen girls, as they are commonly raped and abducted from predators who seek them out online.

Getting to Know Your Teen's Friends: Self-Reflection

△ Do you know all of your teen's closest friends? How often do you see and talk to them? What can you do to get to know your teen's friends more?

△ Do you monitor your teen's social media accounts? Are you familiar with who your teen is befriending online? Do you notice anything inappropriate on your teen's timeline? How can you be more involved in your teen's social media?

_____
_____
_____
_____
_____
_____
_____
_____
_____
_____
_____

Getting to Know Your Teen's Friends: Assignment

△ Make a list of all your teen's closest friends and compare them to all of the items on the previous checklist. Do any of your teen's friends fail to meet the items on this list? If so, how might you address this?

_____
_____
_____
_____
_____
_____
_____
_____
_____
_____
_____
_____
_____
_____

Supporting Your Teen's Emotions

Do you find that your teen feels happy then suddenly sad or frustrated at times for no apparent reason? You might even say that their emotions are "up" and "down". That's because the hormones responsible for puberty—estrogen and progesterone for girls, and testosterone for boys—affect teens emotionally. Not to worry, most teens experience frequent changes in mood as their bodies become flooded with hormones. You might also hear this referred to as mood swings.

Encourage your teen to avoid things that make them irritable. For example, they shouldn't watch television shows or listen to music that make them feel sad or frustrated. Create an environment where your teen is not experiencing high stress at home (i.e., constant fighting or abuse). Also, encourage your teen to do things that naturally improve their mood, such as listening to positive music, writing, drawing, jogging or helping others in need.

Depression and Suicide

Check in with your teen often about how they're feeling. If it seems none of the things that once made them happy interest them anymore or they consistently feel sad, alone or withdrawn, they might be suffering from depression. Other symptoms might include a loss of appetite, wanting to sleep more often, or even making comments about wanting to end their own life.

If your teen ever experiences suicidal thoughts, contact someone right away! The National Suicide Hotline is a great resource that is available to you and your teen with trained professionals who are ready to help 24 hours a day at 1-800-273-8255.

Cutting can also be a sign of depression. Teen girls, especially, resort to cutting in an effort to take their minds off of their problems or release their tension and stress. However, cutting only temporarily distracts them from their problems and can turn into a habit that continues into adulthood. Cutting can also be life-threatening. Accidentally cutting a vein can lead to rapid blood loss, resulting in the loss of consciousness or death.

Ensure your teen that nothing is worth hurting themselves over or taking their own life! No matter how bad things might seem or how bad they might feel, there is always something better for them ahead. Most importantly, let them know that you are there to support them through whatever it is they're going through. Assure your teen that there's no need to be ashamed or embarrassed if they've experienced suicidal thoughts. What's most important is that your teen communicates their feelings so that you can help them get the help they need. You can talk to your teen's school counselor or physician about concerns you have regarding your teen's mental health if you're unsure about where to go.

Stress and Anxiety

Many of the same symptoms described for depression can present themselves if your teen is experiencing anxiety or high stress. Being anxious is normal during circumstances of uncertainty, but the constant feeling of anxiety is not healthy.

High stress can lead to anxiety. This might include feelings of nervousness or feeling jittery. It can also include feelings of intense sadness, frustration, or anger. High stress and anxiety can also cause your teen to act irrationally. Irrational behavior can also be a symptom of substance abuse or a symptom of a personality disorder. Again, talk to your teen about how they're feeling. If they're unsure about their emotions and it causes you concern, seek help from a professional. It is important not to ignore symptoms of depression, anxiety or high stress because they can progress rapidly.

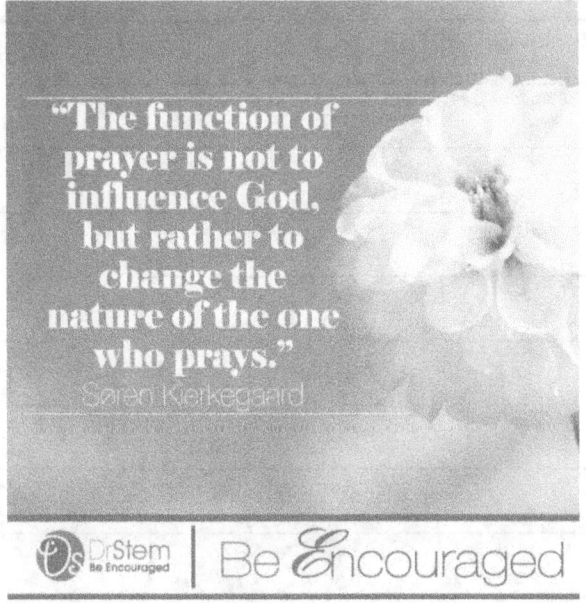

Supporting Your Teen's Emotions? Self- Reflection

△ Have you noticed changes in mood in your teen? What types of things seem to contribute to this? How can you help reduce mood swings in your teen?

△ Has your teen ever demonstrated signs of depression? If so, what did you to address it? What could you have done differently? If not, what can you do to prevent your teen from ever considering suicide?

_____

_____

_____

_____

_____

_____

_____

_____

_____

_____

_____

_____

Supporting Your Teen's Emotions: Assignment

△ Take some time to talk to your teen about their emotions. Ask them what frustrates them most, what makes them sad, and what makes them happiest. Make a list of these things and write down ways you can help discourage the negative items and encourage the positive items.

_____

_____

_____

_____

_____

_____

_____

_____

_____

_____

_____

_____

_____

_____

Love, Dating and Relationships

At this stage, your teen might be curious about love and relationships. This is completely normal for any teenager. They're curious about how they feel about other people and how other people feel about them. They desire to form meaningful relationships and explore love. They might wonder what love really looks like and how they can tell if it's real. Although there's no magic formula for love and relationships, there are key foundational concepts that you can share with your teen to help them navigate through their journey.

Dating: The Point of It All

At this age, your teen might be interested in dating. If they're not interested in dating, or you don't think they're ready to date, it's still a good idea to explain to your teen what it means to date. Dating is all about getting to know someone over time so that, eventually, they can decide if it's a person they'd like to enter into a long-term relationship with. Going out on a date with someone does not mean that they have to be committed to the person forever. It simply means they're interested in getting to know more about the other person—their background, interests, likes and dislikes. It's also a great opportunity to explore what they have in common.

Many people use "dating" and "committed relationships" interchangeably. However, the two should not be confused. Dating is the "getting to know you" phase, whereas a committed relationship is the "we're seeing each other and no one else" phase. A committed relationship might also be solidified by giving each other titles, such as "boyfriend" and "girlfriend".

Unlike a casual dating relationship, a committed relationship is one where two people decide to remain in a relationship with just each other. At this point, they both feel they've gathered all the information they need to know that they have shared interests, love one another, and see a future together long- term. In most cases, couples who enter into a committed relationship have an ultimate goal of marriage. Your teen should not be thinking about getting married anytime soon. They still have a lot to learn about themselves as they continue to mature before they can truly commit themselves to anyone else. However, understanding the difference between a causal dating relationship and a committed relationship can save them a lot of confusion.

How Do I Know When My Teen Is Ready to Date?

There are several signs that will let you know your teen might be ready to date. Some of the things on your checklist should include:

- Your teen is responsible
- Your teen is trustworthy

- Your teen is open and honest about their friends and social life
- Your teen is progressing well in school
- Your teen has a high self-esteem and is not afraid to speak up for his or herself
- Your teen demonstrates strong decision-making skills
- Your teen has a keen understanding of their self-worth
- Your teen is respectful of others
- The person your teen is interested in dating possesses the same qualities outlined above

You might also have additional requirements you want to add to the list. Despite the ability to pass the items on the checklist, some parents are adamant about restricting dating to a certain age. That's ok! It's important that both you and your teen are comfortable with the idea of dating for it to be a positive experience.

If your teen is interested in dating but you're not yet ready, it wouldn't be uncommon for them to think you're being unreasonable. They might even go as far as comparing your decisions to that of their friends' parents. Don't take this personally, and don't be discouraged. Every teenager is different, and some teenagers might be ready to date before others. Remind your teen that you love and care about them, and that you'd much prefer they focus on school without any distractions until you feel they're mature enough to handle the responsibility that comes along with dating. Let your teen know that you will support them in their dating life when the time is right.

Perhaps you're in a situation where you're comfortable with your teen dating but your spouse or co-parent is not. Take some time to create a checklist and establish expectations together. Once you compare your lists, try to reach a consensus. It might also be helpful to share this list with your teen once it's established so they know what your expectations are.

Once your teen is ready to date, make clear to them and the person they're dating what your expectations are. Also, encourage them to choose a place that is safe and that they'll both enjoy. A date should not be in a house alone because they might be tempted to engage in sexual activity if there's no one else around. Public places that allow you them to have fun while getting to know one another are always best. Examples include the movie theatre, your teen's favorite place to eat, or a bowling alley.

How Do I Explain Love to My Teen?

Love can sometimes be difficult to explain, especially to a teenager whose body and brain are still in the development phase. Perhaps you can describe the love you have for your spouse or significant other. You might even use examples of the unconditional love you have for your teen when trying to describe to them what it is. Analogies can also be helpful when trying to provide your teen with an explanation of love.

Love is having a deep affection for someone that comes naturally and is unconditional. Love is much like oxygen. We all need it to survive. Oxygen comes to us naturally. We don't have to create it. Oxygen is always available to us, whether we're up, down, right or wrong. Oxygen is available to us unconditionally and is everlasting. It gives without ever expecting anything in return.

It is very easy to confuse love with emotions that are driven by hormones as a teenager. For example, your teen might be talking to or spending time with someone they really like. They might feel nervous or become excited when they see the person or hear their voice. They might even find themselves thinking about the person often when they're not around.

Explain to your teen that this might mean they're very attracted to the other person, but it doesn't necessarily mean they're in love. Some refer to this as "puppy love"—a phrase people use to describe emotions that mimic love during an early stage of a relationship.

Remind your teen that introducing sex into a dating relationship because they think they're in love is never a good idea.

Remember, sex can produce hormones that send bonding signals to the brain. This makes it difficult for a teen to convince themselves that what they're experiencing is anything but love, when in reality, what they're really experiencing is a longing for the bond or feelings of affection that they've now associated with having sex. This is a concept referred to as lust, not love.

Warn your teen not to never let anyone convince them that sex or any form of mental of physical abuse is a form of love. Being pressured to have sex is never ok, and so is emotional or physical abuse. In fact, these are completely selfish acts, which is the opposite of love because love is unselfish. If your teen feels pressured or abused in any way, they should distance themselves from the person and let you know right away.

Ensure your teen that they have their entire life ahead of them to find the person they want to love for the rest of their life, so there's no rush. For now, they should focus on understanding who they are and preparing themselves for the future.

What if My Teen Experiences Heartbreak?

It's easy for teen's emotions to become involved when dating. This is especially true for teens who are hurt by someone they really like or care about. Feelings of sadness and even anger are normal when this happens.

However, encourage your teen never to blame themselves for anyone else's actions. Teens have a tendency to find fault in themselves when someone has done something to hurt them. They convince themselves that they aren't good enough, popular enough, smart enough, pretty or good looking enough. Warn your teen not to fall into this trap and remind them that they're perfect just the way they are.

If your teen has difficulty getting past the hurt that someone they were dating has caused them, encourage them to focus on things they love to do, rather than spending time replaying what went wrong or trying to figure out what could have been done differently. They might not ever forget, but eventually, they'll get past their feelings of hurt.

In the meantime, encourage them to let go. The more they hold onto their hurt, the longer it will take for them to move past it. Encourage your teen to talk to you about it as much as they need to. If you find that your teen is completely consumed with their feelings of hurt and having great difficulty focusing on anything else, talk to a professional to make sure your teen is not suffering from depression.

What If My Teen Is Unsure About Their Sexual Orientation?

If your teen is unsure about whether they're attracted to the same or opposite sex, this might make them extremely uncomfortable, frustrated or even embarrassed. If your teen shares this with you, don't panic! They might be simply trying to understand their sexual orientation, as they are still learning who they are. If your teen feels certain that they are attracted to the same sex, they might be homosexual—gay or lesbian. If they're attracted to both girls and guys, they might be bisexual.

This doesn't mean that anything is wrong with your teen, and you shouldn't be afraid. It might take several more years of learning about themselves before they truly understand their sexual orientation. However, if they are certain about their sexuality, try not to add to their frustration or fear by lashing out at them.

Instead, talk to your teen about their assessment of their sexual orientation, how it makes them feel, and how you can best support them. If your personal views make it hard for you to do this, involve a trusted mentor or professional in the conversation. Admitting to a sexual orientation that is generally not socially accepted can be extremely hard for a teen and can severely impact their self-esteem. They need to know that they can trust you and that you love them, no matter what.

Love, Dating and Relationships: Self-Reflection

- What was your understanding of love and dating as a teenager? Did anyone talk to you about what it was? Is there anything you wish you had known about it as a teen that you didn't learn until later in life?

- Has your teen expressed interest in dating? How does your teen dating make you feel?

How does your teen compare to the checklist for identifying whether or not your teen is ready to date?

_____
_____
_____
_____
_____
_____
_____
_____
_____
_____
_____

Love, Dating and Love, Dating and Relationships: Assignment

△ Take time to talk to your teen about what love is. Ask them what loves means to them and share what love looks like compared to lust. Describe the difference between a casual dating relationship and a committed relationship. Ask your teen what type of "data" they'd want to collect from a person when going on a date to determine if they're a good fit. Create a list together and make it fun!

_____
_____
_____
_____
_____
_____
_____
_____
_____
_____
_____
_____

Supporting Your Teen's Goals

One way to help your teen avoid many of the distractions that might negatively affect them is to encourage them to set their sights on their personal goals. Having a clear understanding of what they want to achieve in life and outlining steps that require their focus will set them up for success!

What Is A Personal Goal?

Personal goals are goals that a person sets for themselves. No one else can set them for you. Your teen might not be completely sure about what they want for their future, but they likely have some idea of what they'd like to accomplish. At a bare minimum, they can identify what might make them happy in life.

Your teen's personal goals can be as big or as small as they want them to be, as long as they are meaningful to them.

These goals can be things they hope to accomplish by next month or within the next 5 years. Examples of personal goals might include achieving a certain number of steps per day, learning how to speak another language, being accepted into the college or their choice, or becoming a professional in what they consider to be their dream job.

Setting goals might sound like a simple concept, but it takes discipline to complete the necessary steps to achieve them. It's not enough for your teen to say they want to achieve something without actually taking actions toward making it happen. Talk to your teen about what their personal goals are and give them positive feedback. Help your teen to outline steps to achieve their goals and support them however you can. Most times, being their biggest "cheerleader" or fan is more than enough.

Helping your teen to monitor their goals doesn't require any type of formal tracking process. There's no need to develop fancy charts or create calculated measures. Make it fun! Help your teen to track their goals in a way that will keep them engaged. This can be in the form of a colorful checklist they create in their favorite notebook or even a vision board with pictures that reflect what your teen is trying to achieve.

Talk to your teen often about progress with their goals, including setbacks. Make clear to your teen that failure doesn't mean they're not good enough or smart enough to be successful. Let them know that setbacks can provide them with valuable lessons to help them achieve their goals in the future. This will help deter your teen from being easily discouraged.

Provide your teen with positive reinforcement by celebrating small successes. The more motivated they are about achieving their goal, the less likely they are to get distracted. Teens with no goals in mind are more likely to fall victim to many of the peer pressures that can jeopardize their future.

Be careful not to impose your own goals upon your teen. You want the best for your teen, and it's ok to have big dreams for their future. However, it's important to remember that your teen is an individual. What you have in mind for their future might not be in line with their passions and interests. Failure to recognize this can put pressure on your teen to please you, despite what they want for themselves. You can prevent your teen from experiencing this type of stress by actively supporting the goals they have outlined for themselves.

Tips for Helping Your Teen Achieve Their Goals

Here are a few tips that you can share with your teen for setting goals and working toward them:

- Stay true to yourself. Don't set goals based on what others think you should do (or what everyone else seems to be doing).

- Believe in yourself. You are smart enough, brave enough and capable enough to do anything you set your mind to.

- Make your goals achievable. Try not to set the bar so high that you set yourself up for failure. Start small and gradually expand upon the goals you have for yourself.

- Don't rush. Be diligent and take your time.

- Adjust plans for achieving your goals when necessary. It's ok to make changes.

- Stay committed. Don't back out of a goal that you've set for yourself because you miss the mark a few times.

- Share your goals with family and friends so that they can support you. If your friends make fun of your goals, they are not friends who have your best interest in mind. Surround yourself with friends who are positive and supportive.

Supporting a College Bound Teen

If your teen is interested in attending college, this can be an exciting time! It's never too early to begin discussing with your teen what college they want to attend and what they're interested in studying.

Talk to your teen about what they want to do to support themselves for a living. Ask them what type of career they envision and why. This information will help your teen decide whether or not the field of study they have in mind is really in line with what they want to do. Once you narrow down the area of focus, begin looking into colleges that specialize in this area and try to arrange as many college tours as you possibly can. Where physical tours are not possible, take time to review their websites, reviews and available videos. If you know of anyone who attended any of these colleges, arrange time for your teen to speak with them about their experience.

Once you've done the necessary research, work with your teen to narrow the colleges that interest them to their top 5. Then, begin looking into the admissions process, requirements and available scholarship opportunities for each of them. This will allow you to assess your teen's current grades and achievements compared to what's required and work on areas where your teen might need improvement.

It's best to start the process early, even as much as a year or two before graduation. If your teen waits until their senior year to begin their search, it won't leave them much time to work toward achieving the necessary requirements. It also won't leave you much time to help your teen prepare financially.

Hopefully, you are already saving for your teen's future. If not, now is a good time to start. The best-case scenario would be that your teen receives scholarship money to support their college education. However, often times, financial assistance is needed, whether it comes from you or a government loan. The fact is, college comes with a financial commitment, not just to cover the cost of tuition, but to cover the cost of books, supplies and living (i.e., dorm, apartment, food, gas).

Preparing Your Teen for College

When the time comes for your teen to start college, develop a checklist of everything they might need to be successful and live comfortably. This includes school supplies, personal supplies and home goods if your teen will be staying on campus or in an apartment.

Review the expectations you have of your teen while they're away. For example, you might require them to call you once a day or update you weekly on their spending if you're supporting them financially. Even if your teen plans to remain in the home with you while attending a local college, setting clear expectations is important. For example, will your teen have an extended curfew now that they're in college? Are they now expected to contribute to their cell phone bill? Are they expected to work part-time?

In setting your expectations for college life, make sure that they are realistic and reasonable. Remember that this is an important time for your teen to exercise independence. This means you'll need to learn how to "let go". This is a time for your teen to exercise skills such as decision making and critical thinking both inside and outside of the classroom. They won't be able to do this if you try to control every move they make. Try your best to fight the urge to run to their rescue for everything. They won't always get it right, but even their mistakes will prepare them for the real world. This isn't easy to do, but it's necessary to their development and transition into adulthood.

If your teen is going away for college, you might find it hard to adjust to them not being inside of the home. Your spouse and/or siblings might also struggle with this. It's perfectly normal to miss seeing your teen around the house every day. This might even sadden you for a bit. However, there are many ways to stay connected with your teen even while they're away. In addition to visiting, you can schedule time to talk with them by phone or maintain constant contact through social media or videoconferencing apps. Even then, communication with your teen might be limited because they have classes to take, studying to do and a social life. So, try not to take their limited availability personally.

What If My Teen is Not Interested in College?

Not every teenager is interested in attending college after graduating high school. This doesn't mean your teen doesn't have what it takes or that they're an underachiever; it simply means that a traditional college experience might not be right for them. If this is the case with your teen, revisit their goals with them and determine if trade school or a special certification is best. Completing college courses online is also becoming an increasingly popular option.

If you're unsure about the type of degree or certification your teen might need to excel at what they want to do as a career, talk with a school counselor. There are also several free youth programs run by nonprofit organizations that offer this type of guidance. Talk to some of the youth organizations within your community about what resources they might be able to offer.

Supporting Your Teen's Personal Goals: Self-Reflection

△ What goals do you have for your teen? Are you aware of your teen's personal goals? Are your teen's goals in line with yours?

△ Have you begun talking with your teen about college or what they envision as a career? Are you comfortable with your teen going away for college or would you prefer that they stay close to home? What can you do to help your teen financially prepare for a college education?

_____
_____
_____
_____
_____
_____
_____
_____
_____
_____
_____
_____

Supporting Your Teen's Personal Goals: Assignment

△ Ask your teen to describe their ideal career. Talk to them about what it might take to be successful in this career, then make a list of things they can begin doing now to achieve this success. Help your teen create a vision board with a timeline of when they might achieve each step outlined on the list. Include pictures of some of their colleges of interest.

_____
_____
_____
_____
_____
_____
_____
_____
_____
_____
_____

Raising Teen Girls

The same hormones that are responsible for your teenage girl's emotions are responsible for her changing body. Her brain releases a special hormone called gonadotropin-releasing hormone, also known as GnRH. Simply put, when this hormone reaches the pituitary gland, which is the gland just under the brain, the hormones responsible for puberty kick in. For girls, this means a significant amount of estrogen and progesterone.

Physical Appearance

You might notice that certain areas of your teen's body are filling out more. For example, she might not be able to get away with not wearing a bra anymore or she may have outgrown her current bra size. Maybe her jeans fit a little tighter in the hip and butt area. She might also notice hair appear on several parts of her body. Encourage your teen not to panic or feel awkward about her changing appearance. These types of changes are completely normal during puberty.

Your teen's skin is no exception to hormonal changes. This is especially true with acne. Acne is also triggered by your teen's changing hormones and causes the sebaceous glands, which are the oil glands, to enlarge and overproduce oil. This causes your teen's skin to become inflamed and can result in blemishes and pimples. Acne can also present itself on the shoulders, back, neck, chest and upper arms. If your teen can't seem to get her acne under control, talk to a physician about the best solution for her skin.

A few tips for maintaining clear skin include, drinking plenty of water, washing and moisturizing the face once or twice daily, and using mild cleansers without fragrances that irritate the skin. If your teen uses makeup, encourage her not to apply too much and to use makeup that is breathable. Your teen should also use the proper makeup remover for her skin.

DIETING

It is common for teens girls to struggle with their weight during this stage. Teen girls are especially drawn to the concept of dieting if they think their weight is not ideal. Some girls take dieting too far and decide not to eat at all. Explain to your teen that depriving her body of the nutrients it needs is never a good idea. In fact, her body needs all of the nutrients it can get during this stage of her life.

Some teen girls go through great lengths to put weight on to achieve a certain shape or figure. This can also lead to unhealthy eating practices. Unless her doctor tells her to change her diet in any way, encourage her not to attempt any "fad" diets simply because they appear to be popular.

Weight gain during puberty is completely normal, and so is weight loss. What's most important is that your teen is healthy. This means eating healthy and exercising at least 30 minutes a day.

Self-Image

Teen girls can be incredibly consumed with how they look based on other people's opinions. You might notice that your teen is paying more attention to her size, height, hair color and style of her clothes. This is because she wants to fit in by gaining the acceptance of others.

Many teen girls try to imitate what they see on television or social media. Unfortunately, this can often times lead them to wear revealing or "sexy" clothing. Explain to your teen that clothing that is too revealing can sometimes draw the wrong type of attention from guys. Guys might assume that she wants to draw attention to herself that is sexual in nature simply based on how she's dressed.

Remind your teen that what others think of her doesn't matter. What's important is that she always remain true to who she is. In fact, being unique is what makes her special. Explain to her that those who are worth being in her life will appreciate her just for who she is.

Menstrual Cycles

By now, your teen might have already experienced her menstrual cycle, also referred to as a "period". If she hasn't experienced it yet, it will be here before she knows it. Ensure her that menstruating is nothing to be afraid of. In fact, it's completely healthy and natural.

A girl's menstrual cycle is her body's way of preparing for a pregnancy each month and typically lasts anywhere between 21 to 45 days. This doesn't mean she'll actually bleed this number of days. Menstrual bleeding typically lasts no more than a week.

Menstrual bleeding can vary from person to person. Your teen might wonder how long her menstrual bleeding should last. Although menstrual bleeding typically lasts for about a week, it is possible for the number of days to vary from month to month. It is also possible to experience lighter or heavier flows from month to month. While some teens experience a regular cycle that allows them to anticipate when their menstrual bleeding will begin, others experience irregular cycles which makes it harder to pinpoint when their menstrual bleeding will begin.

Your teen might also experience different comfort levels with various feminine products. Tell her not to be discouraged. Help your teen to take her time finding products that suit her needs in terms of comfort and flow.

A cycle is counted from the first day of one period to the first day of the next period.

About halfway through your teen's cycle, her ovaries release an egg which travels down her fallopian tubes to be fertilized by a sperm. Her hormones begin to rise and the lining in her uterus begins to thicken. This is a process known as ovulation.

Pregnancy happens if the egg is fertilized by a man's sperm and attaches to the uterine wall. If the egg is not fertilized, it will break apart. This causes your teen's hormone levels to drop and the thickened lining of the uterus to "melt away". When this happens, the lining exits her body in the form of blood. Her body will repeat this process every month, unless she is taking a birth control pill designed to prevent a regular cycle.

Remember, having a menstrual cycle is completely natural. However, if your teen experiences unbearable pain or abnormally heavy bleeding, bring it to the attention of a physician. Also, encourage your teen to track the start of her menstrual cycles from one month to next and make note of any major changes.

Tips to Help Your Teen Girl Embrace Her Changing Body

Remind your teen that none of the changes her body is experiencing make her any less beautiful! The fact that her body is maturing is beautiful in itself.

So, what can you share with your teen to help her adjust to all of these changes? Here are a few tips to share with her.

- Δ Wear clothing that you feel comfortable in. Whether you enjoy walking around the mall with your friends or actively playing sports, shop for undergarments (i.e., bras, underwear) that feel good on. Don't settle on a bra or underwear simply because it looks cute.

- Δ Eat healthy and exercise at least 30 minutes a day.

- Δ Try not to overcompensate for your acne with makeup. Too much makeup can actually clog your pores. What your skin needs most is oxygen and water.

∆ Get plenty of rest. Being well rested improves your overall mood.

∆ Remind yourself of how beautiful you are. Focus on the things you love about yourself. Try not be get distracted by anything else.

∆ If a first you don't succeed at finding a feminine product that works best for you, try, try again.

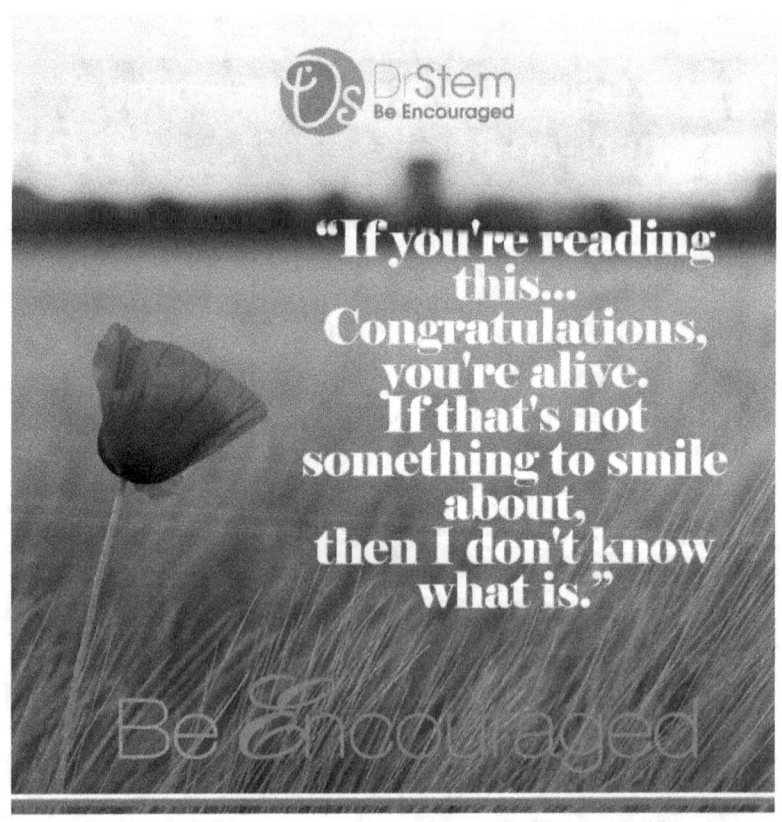

Raising Teen Boys

The same hormones that produce estrogen in girls are responsible for producing testosterone in boys. Like girls, boys will undergo several physical changes—some of which are the same, and some of which are drastically different.

Physical Appearance

Teen boys typically grow taller during this stage. They also grow more facial hair, hair under the arms, on the arms and legs, and on the groin area. Although acne impacts all teens regardless of their sex, it can especially impact teen boys if they are engaged in sports.

Constant sweating can worsen the overproduction of the oil glands, making it harder to keep acne under control. Encourage your teen to practice good hygiene habits such as washing his face up to twice a day with a mild cleanser. Drinking plenty of water will also help.

This is also the stage when teen boys increase their weight and muscle mass. Teen boys tend to be consumed with how muscular they are during this stage because of the social expectation that "real men" are strong and have lots of muscles. This might peak your teen's interest in protein powders, shakes, and other dietary supplements designed to help build muscle mass. However, like any other supplement, talk to your teen's physician about any dietary changes.

Your teen's sexual organs are also growing larger. Unfortunately, like muscle mass, teen boys undergo the pressure of comparing the size of their sexual organs to that of their peers because they associate the size of their sexual organs with their sense of manhood. Even teen girls make reference to the size of a boy's sexual organs as a symbolism of how strong or attractive they are. However, teen boys' sexual organs grow to be different sizes as a different pace. Explain to your teen that the size of his body or sexual organs does not define him as a man.

Sex and Hormones

At this stage, teen boys are able to ejaculate (release sperm). This can happen even in their sleep. This is also a stage when boys can easily become consumed with the thought of sex. Remember, we live in a culture where sex is portrayed as the ultimate pleasure. In addition to cultural influences, raging hormones can cause teen boys to easily become aroused. This natural state of arousal might even lead them to pleasure or "relief" themselves.

If your teen finds it hard to keep his mind off of sex, encourage him to occupy his time with things he enjoys doing. If your teen has too much time on his hands, he might begin to engage in sex as a recreational sport.

Masculinity, Self-Image and Social Expectations

It is common for teen boys to associate physical appearance and social status with masculinity. This is in large part due to the culture that we live in, especially the media. Movies and television are notorious for portraying men as being strong with muscles, likeable and having lots of power. Even popular superheroes fit this bill.

The music that teenage boys listen to is also filled with messages of physical attributes and sexual stamina as prerequisites of manhood. Music lyrics can be very explicit these days.

For example, lyrics often tie being able to "last all night" or "stroke" in a certain manner to masculinity. Our culture also portrays having multiple women and dominating over them as a symbolism of power. This can impact how your teen addresses women and his role as a man in a relationship.

Teen boys are also subject to a culture of being "tough"—the notion that "real men" don't back down or show emotion.

Unfortunately, this can prevent teen boys from opening up and cause them to shut down because they're afraid of being perceived as too sensitive or "weak". This stereotype can also lead to overly expressing feelings of aggression. For example, if someone picks a fight with your teen at school while everyone is watching, he might feel an enormous pressure to prove his masculinity by being physically aggressive.

Aggression in teen boys is natural due to their hormones. However, being overly aggressive is not a good sign. Stressful circumstances, such as an unstable home or difficulty in school can also contribute to your teen's aggression. Try getting him involved in a physical sport or encourage him to engage in physical exercise often to help with this. You might spend some time running with him a few times a week, which can also help you to bond.

There are a multitude of things can impact how your teen perceives what is expected of him as a man. Talk to your teen often about his place in the world and as a man. Explain to him that men can be nurturers as much as they are protectors and providers of those they love.

Encourage them to open up as much as needed about their feelings, even if it makes them feel vulnerable. Let your teen know that he is human and is not expected to be a superhero. A real superhero is one who is responsible, works hard, and respectful of those around him.

If you are a single parent without any male figures in your teen's life, identify male figures who you trust and can positively influence your teen. This can be a grandparent, uncle, spiritual leader, teacher or coach. Arrange for your teen to spend time with these role models so that he is comfortable talking to them and asking for advice.

There will be so many times you will feel like you've failed. But even though they do not show it often, in the eyes and heart of your teen you are a super parent. Be Encouraged

Single Parenting

You may be raising your children on your own. Being a single parent can be challenging. It can also be very rewarding. You may be a single parent due to divorce or death of a partner. Maybe you are parenting alone by choice. Being a single parent doesn't mean you're alone. You may have family members, friends, or neighbors nearby that can pitch in when you need them. The key is asking and being open to receiving help from others around you. You can also find a support group for single parents in your community, church or neighborhood.

Look to your local community centers and religious organizations to see the groups they offer. You'll meet other people who are in similar situations. Participating in a support group gives you a chance to share your feelings and get advice.

Being a single parent can cause financial strain. You may have problems finding childcare. The life of a single parent can be very busy. In addition to taking care of your children and your home, you may also be working and/or going to school. It's important to find a way to balance all of the parts of your life. There are things you can do so you don't feel overwhelmed. Here are some ways to help you cope with being a single parent:

Accept help. If friends and family offer their help, take it! This can mean having someone play stay with your teen, help your teen with school work or stand in for you at meetings and games. Call a friend, family member to talk and get relief when you are overwhelmed. If you are in an area with counselors and you have health insurance, accept and allow yourself to see a counselor for support.

Take advantage of local resources. Every employer also has a program called EAP-Employee Assistance Program, which is great program that has counselors you can talk to for free about parenting teens, work stress, illness. The program is a Free program that also has services like counseling for your teen.

Make time for your teen. Find creative ways to spend more time with your teen, because even though they make it like they don't care, they do. See if your job will let you work flexible hours and make dates with your teen, even if it is a consistent 2 hours a week. They just want to know more of you and from you.

Have some me time and fun. Take a break from your busy routine to plan something special for you.

Stay active. Exercise is good all around. Find ways for you and your teen to work out, walk, or do their favorite exercise. I know trying is also good enough because the goal here is for you to have the opportunity to connect with them.

Parenting is hard work. All parents have times when they get angry or frustrated. But try not to take out your feelings on your child. If you start to feel overwhelmed, ask for help right away. Telling your child negative information in any way, shape or form is damaging to your teen. There are now in person and social media support groups around the world you can join. Never feel alone. Join the groups for more support.

Overcoming the Challenges of Co-Parenting

Co-parenting after a split is rarely easy, especially if you have a contentious relationship with your ex-partner. You may be concerned about your ex's parenting abilities, stressed about child support or other financial issues, his new woman, feel worn down by conflict, or think you'll never be able to overcome all the resentments in your relationship. But co-parenting amicably with your ex can give your children especially teenagers the stability, security, and close relationships with both parents they need. Especially for the sake of your teenager's well-being, it is important for you to overcome co-parenting challenges and develop a cordial working relationship with your ex. With these tips, you can remain calm, stay consistent, and resolve conflicts to make joint custody work and enable your teens to excel and thrive. I will refer to teenager's however, this information pertains to all your children even younger.

Understanding co-parenting

Unless your family has faced serious issues such as domestic violence or substance abuse, co-parenting—having both parents play an active role in their teenager's daily lives—is the best way to ensure all your teenager's needs are met and they are able to retain close relationships with both parents. Research suggests that the quality of the relationship between co-parents can also have a strong influence on the mental and emotional well-being of all their children, and the incidence of anxiety and depression. Of course, putting aside relationship issues, especially after a bitter and hostile split, to co-parent agreeably can be easier said than done.

Joint custody arrangements can be exhausting, infuriating, and very stressful. It can be extremely difficult to get past the painful history you may have with your ex and overcome built-up resentments. Making shared decisions, interacting with each other at drop-offs, or just speaking to a person you'd rather forget all about can seem like impossible tasks.

Despite the many challenges, though, it is possible to develop an amicable working relationship with your ex for the sake of your children. I always suggest parents seek help dealing with all the emotions that come up with co-parenting. I provide video and telephone coaching which really helps ease the emotional part of this journey as it is not easy to emotionally deal with the anger, frustration and resentment that goes with co-parenting. My booking information is at the end of this book.

Making co-parenting work

The key to successful co-parenting is to separate the personal relationship with your ex from the co-parenting relationship. It may be helpful to start thinking of your relationship with your ex as a completely new one—one that is entirely about the well-being of your children, and not about either of you. Your marriage may be over, but your family is not; doing what is best for your kids is your most important priority.

The important step to being a loving, mature, responsible co-parent is to always put your children's needs especially teenagers ahead of your own. It is not easy however the benefit of having emotional strong able and capable teens is priceless. Their success is your success. You and their mom/ dad's ability to make the relationship easier for them to be between the two homes makes it easier for them to deal with the teen years and your separation or divorce.

Benefits for your children

Through your co-parenting partnership, your teens need to recognize that they are more important than the conflict that ended your marriage—and understand that your love for them will prevail despite changing circumstances. Their first thought even as teens is that they were a part of the discord that caused the divorce. They feel justified when they are always caught in between and parents are unable to agree on their well being. Cooperation with your ex is beneficial to your teen as follows:

- **Feel secure.** When confident of the love of both parents, teens adjust more quickly and easily to divorce and new living situations and have better self-esteem and self-confidence. They are not easily influenced to use drugs, drink, smoke to suppress the pain they feel when parents are not in agreement. Most kids turn to drugs, alcohol, prostitution, smoking to numb the pain of dealing with parents who are not getting along, even as adult children the resentment between parents is difficult to deal with. Depression and anxiety can also be the result of the inability to feel secure when parents are not in cooperation.
- **Benefit from consistency.** Co-parenting fosters similar rules, discipline, and rewards between households,

so children know what to expect, and what's expected of them.
- **Better understand problem solving.** Children who see their parents continuing to work together are more likely to learn how to effectively and peacefully solve problems themselves.
- **Have a healthy example to follow.** By cooperating with the other parent, you are establishing a life pattern your children can carry into the future to build and maintain stronger relationships.
- **Are mentally and emotionally healthier.** Children exposed to conflict between co-parents are more likely to develop issues such as depression, anxiety, or ADHD.

Setting hurt and anger aside

Successful co-parenting means that your own emotions—any anger, resentment, or hurt—must take a back seat to the needs of your children. I know it is not fair, it is not. However, Undoubtedly, setting aside such strong feelings may be the very hard, but it's also perhaps the most important thing that your teenager needs. Co-parenting is unfortunately not about your feelings, or those of your ex-spouse, but rather about your child's happiness, stability, and future well-being.

Separating feelings from behavior

It's okay to be hurt and angry, but your feelings don't have to dictate your behavior. Instead, let what's best for your teen motivate your actions. Sacrificing your all for a teen at times does not appear worthy because of the natural teenage personality, behavior and unappreciated behaviors.

Your complete loving and caring involvement and sacrifice is the one major positive thing that will help your teenager make it through these challenging teen years.

Get your feelings out somewhere else. Never vent to your child. Friends, therapists, coaches like myself, or even a loving pet can all make good listeners when you need to get negative feelings off your chest. Exercise can also be a healthy outlet for letting off steam.

Stay Centered and Focused on your teen's wellness. If you feel angry or resentful, try to remember why you need to act with purpose and grace: your teen's best interests are at stake. If your anger feels overwhelming, looking at a photograph of your teen as a child may help you calm down.

Don't put your children in the middle

You may never completely lose all of your resentment or bitterness about your break up, but what you can do is sort out those feelings and remind yourself that they are your issues, not your child's. Resolve to keep your issues with your ex away from your children. Many teenagers are caught up in the middle of the resentment between their parents or adults in their lives, that they find it difficult to function or survive at times. I emphasize this as I have worked with many teenagers whose primarily struggle, anger or sadness was because of the resentment or disagreements that happened between their parents. They hear and see everything, I mean everything.

Never use your teens as messengers. When you use your teens or children in general to convey messages to your co-parent, it puts them in the center of your conflict. The goal is to keep your child out of your relationship issues, so call or email your ex directly. It is easier for your emotions to be so strong that you at times wish the children were never born because you wouldn't be going through all these troubles, so try not to let your teen know or feel this feeling you are feeling. They react negatively and take everything seriously at heart. They hurt and feel like they are the trouble. They feel they are not wanted and many times express their wish to die and end their parent's misery.

Keep your issues to yourself. Never say negative things about your ex to your teen, or make them feel like they have to choose. Your teen has a right to a relationship with their other parent that is free of your influence. Allow them the space to be happy in the presence of both parents. Being flexible with visits and requests from the other co-parent is a gift to your children and it doesn't mean they love the other parent more. To the children it is never about who is the better parent, they just love being with either of you at all times. They just want the continued connection with mom and dad.

Improving communication with your co-parent

Peaceful, consistent, and purposeful communication with your ex is essential to the success of co-parenting—even though it may seem absolutely impossible. **It all begins with your mindset. Think about communication with your ex as having the highest purpose: your child's well-being.** Before contact with your ex, ask yourself how your talk will affect your child, and find ways you can conduct yourself with dignity and calmness. When you change the way you see and look at any situation or anything, the things you look at change and the situations indeed changes as well. Make your wellbeing, peace of mind, your teen's wellbeing and success the focal point of every discussion you have with your ex-partner.

Remember that it isn't always necessary to meet your ex in person—speaking over the phone or exchanging texts or emails is fine for the majority of conversations. The goal is to establish conflict-free communication, so see which type of contact works best for you.

Co-parenting communication methods

However you choose to communicate, the following methods can help you initiate and maintain effective stress free communication:

Set a business-like tone. Approach the relationship with your ex as a business partnership where your "business" is your children's well-being. Speak or write to your ex as you would a colleague—with cordiality, respect, and neutrality. Relax and talk slowly.

Make requests. Instead of making statements, which can be misinterpreted as demands, try framing as much as you can as requests. Requests can begin "Would you be willing to...?" or "Can we try...?"

Listen. Communicating with maturity starts with listening. Breath while you listen. Close your eyes, breath in slowly through your nose and blow out slowly through your mouth, breath. Many parents forget to breath and end up themselves with stress induced illnesses and problems.

Even if you end up disagreeing with the other parent, you should at least be able to convey to your ex that you've understood their point of view. And listening does not signify approval, so you won't lose anything by allowing your ex to voice his or her opinions.

Respond Not React Keep in mind that communicating with one another is going to be necessary for the length of your teenager's entire childhood—if not longer. You can train yourself to Respond that is not overreact to your ex, and over time you can become numb to the buttons they try to push. Responding means you get angry, upset, irritable with your ex each time you communicate with him/her.

Commit to meeting/talking consistently. Though it may be extremely difficult in the early stages, frequent communication with your ex will convey the message to your children that you and your co-parent are a united front.

Keep conversations kid-focused. Never let a discussion with your ex-partner stray into a conversation about your needs or their needs; it should always be about your child's needs only.

Quickly relieve stress in the moment. It may seem impossible to stay calm when dealing with a difficult ex-spouse who's hurt you in the past or has a real knack for pushing your buttons. If you're truly ready to rebuild trust after a break up, be sincere about your efforts. Remember your children's best interests as you move forward to improve your relationship. Look good, feel good to make easier to deal with the new changes as you co parent.

- **Ask your ex's opinion.** This simple technique can jump-start positive communications between you. Take an issue that you don't feel strongly about, and ask for your ex's input, showing that you value their input.
- **Apologize.** When you're sorry about something, apologize sincerely—even if the incident happened a long time ago. Apologizing can be very powerful in moving your relationship away from being adversaries.
- **Chill out.** If a special outing with your ex is going to cut into your time with your child by an hour, graciously let it be. Remember that it's all about what is best for your child. Plus, when you show flexibility, your ex is more likely to be flexible with you and your children will be even more grateful of the time.

Co-parenting as a team

Parenting is full of decisions you'll have to make with your ex, whether you like each other or not. Cooperating and communicating without blow-ups or bickering makes decision-making far easier on everybody. If you shoot for consistency, cordiality, and teamwork with your co-parent, the details of child-rearing decisions tend to fall into place.

Aim for co-parenting consistency

It's healthy for children to be exposed to different perspectives and to learn to be flexible, but they also need to know they're living under the same basic set of expectations at each home. Aiming for consistency between your home and your ex's avoids confusion for your children. Please note: you can no longer have input into who or what your ex does at their home. Express a concern and know that the other parent has the right to provide and parent their way when the children are in their home, as long as it is safe for him/her to do so.

Rules. Rules don't have to be exactly the same between two households, but if you and your ex-spouse establish generally consistent guidelines, your kids won't have to bounce back and forth between two radically different disciplinary environments. Important lifestyle rules like homework issues, curfews, and off-limit activities should be followed in both households.

Discipline. Try to follow similar systems of consequences for broken rules, even if the infraction didn't happen under your roof. So, if your kids have lost TV privileges while at your ex's house, follow through with the restriction. The same can be done for rewarding good behavior.

Schedule. Where you can, aim for some consistency in your children's schedules. Making meals, homework, and bedtimes similar can go a long way toward your child's adjustment to having two homes.

Making important decisions as co-parents

Major decisions need to be made by both you and your ex. Being open, honest, and straightforward about important issues is crucial to both your relationship with your ex and your children's well-being.

Medical needs. Whether you decide to designate one parent to communicate primarily with health care professionals or attend medical appointments together, keep one another in the loop.

Education. Be sure to let the school know about changes in your child's living situation. Speak with your ex ahead of time about class schedules, extra-curricular activities, and parent-teacher conferences, and be polite to each other at school or sports events.

Financial issues. The cost of maintaining two separate households can strain your attempts to be effective co-parents. Set a realistic budget and keep accurate records for shared expenses. Be gracious if your ex provides opportunities for your children that you cannot provide.

Resolving co-parenting disagreements

As you co-parent, you and your ex are bound to disagree over certain issues. Keep the following in mind as you try to reach a consensus.

Respect can go a long way. Simple manners should be the foundation for co-parenting. Being considerate and respectful includes letting your ex know about school events, being flexible about your schedule when possible, and taking their opinion seriously.

Keep talking. If you disagree about something important, you will need to continue communicating. Never discuss your differences of opinions with or in front of your child. If you still can't agree, you may need to talk to a third party, like a therapist or mediator.

Don't sweat the small stuff. If you disagree about important issues like a medical surgery or choice of school for your child, by all means keep the discussion going. But if you want your child in bed by 7:30 and your ex says 8:00, let it go and save your energy for the bigger issues.

Compromise. Yes, you will need to come around to your ex spouse's point of view as often as he or she comes around to yours. It may not always be your first choice, but compromise allows you both to "win" and makes both of you more likely to be flexible in the future.

Make transitions and visitation easier

The actual move from one household to another, whether it happens every few days or just certain weekends, can be a very hard time for children. Every reunion with one parent is also a separation with the other, each "hello" also a "goodbye." While transitions are unavoidable, there are many things you can do to help make them easier on your children.

When your child leaves

As kids prepare to leave your house for your ex's, try to stay positive and deliver them on time.

Help children anticipate change. Remind kids they'll be leaving for the other parent's house a day or two before the visit.

Pack in advance. Depending on their age, even teens might need help. Help them pack their bags well before they leave so that they don't forget anything they'll miss. Encourage packing familiar reminders like a special stuffed toy or photograph with your younger kids.

Always drop off—never pick up the child. It's a good idea to avoid "taking" your child from the other parent so that you don't risk interrupting or curtailing a special moment. Drop off your teen at the other parent's house instead.

When your child returns

The beginning of your teen's return to your home can be awkward or even rocky. To help your teen adjust:

Keep things low-key. When your teen first enters your home, try to have some down time together, or allow them to go into their room which they most likely will do. They might just want a hi and bye small talk. That is ok—read a book, cook, clean or do some other quiet activity until they are ready to talk.

Double up. To make packing simpler and make your teen feel more comfortable when they are at the other parent's house, have them keep certain basics—toothbrush, hairbrush, pajamas—at both houses.

Allow your teen space. Teenagers often need a little time to adjust to the transition. If they seem to need some space, allow them the space. In time, things will get back to normal.

Establish a special routine. Play a game or serve the same special meal each time your child returns. Teens thrive on routine—if they know exactly what to expect when they return to you it can help the transition.

Dealing with visitation refusal

It's common that kids in joint custody sometimes refuse to leave one parent to be with the other.

- **Find the cause.** The problem may be one that is easy to resolve, like paying more attention to your child, making a change in discipline style, or having more toys if younger kids or other entertainment. Or it may be that an emotional reason is at hand, such as conflict or misunderstanding. Talk to your teen about their refusal. Teenagers are very sensitive. They want to be involved in the decision making especially where and when they can stay longer with one parent or both. Engage them and hear their side.
- **Go with the flow.** Whether you have detected the reason for the refusal or not, try to give your child the space and time that they obviously need. It may have nothing to do with you at all. And take heart: most cases of visitation refusal are temporary.
- **Talk to your ex.** A heart-to-heart with your ex about the refusal may be challenging and emotional but can help you figure out what the problem is. Try to be sensitive and understanding to your ex as you discuss this touchy subject. Again it is for your teen emotional and mental stability as well their peace of mind and happiness.

Affirmational Thoughts and Next Steps

△ Now that you've completed this book, write down some positive thoughts you have about your journey of parenting a teen. What are you feeling more confident or optimistic about?

△ What are your biggest takeaways? Place a sticky note on the pages that correlate with these takeaways as a reminder that you have a resource handy if a similar situation presents itself.

_____
_____
_____
_____
_____
_____
_____
_____
_____
_____
_____
_____

Let's Connect

Join Dr. Stem on Face Book Live on Tuesday evenings for discussions on topics discussed in this book and more.

Enroll in Parent & Teen Empowerment Webinars and online courses, and connect with other teenagers around the world for moral support, fun and encouragement.

All online programs are on:
https://www.drstemmie.com/

Look out for the Parent & Teen Empowerment Conference or Workshop coming to your city, a city near you or at sea.

Inquire at drstem14@gmail.com

About the Author

Originally from Zimbabwe, Africa, Dr. Sithembile "Stem" Mahlatini is president and owner of Global Counseling & Coaching Services, in Orlando, Florida, and she is also president and founder of Parent & Teen Empowerment Conference & Parent & Teen Empowerment Seminars. She is a certified life-career coach, author, licensed psychotherapist and motivational/inspirational speaker. She resides in Orlando, Florida USA.

Dr. Stem's life's work is to inspire, motivate and educate others through her books, seminars, workshops, and Counseling and Coaching Services. Drawing on her background as a licensed psychotherapist, life- career coach, speaker and author, she offers people practical advice on how to tap into their limitless power to change their lives, overcome roadblocks and aspire to be better than the circumstances that surround them. Her life-long goal is to continue to empower and inspire teenagers, parents, and couples to be winners at home, work and business. Her motto is, "Each day is an opportunity to change your life and bring out the new you."

Dr. Mahlatini attended Nova Southeastern University where she earned a doctorate degree in education, specializing in organizational leadership. She is also a graduate of Boston University, where she earned a master's degree in social work, and she is licensed as a psychotherapist in Massachusetts and Florida. She is a member of the Back Talk Toastmasters club, the Professional Woman Network, and the National Association of Social Workers.

Listen to DrStem weekly on The DrStem Show on https://americaoutloud.com/show/the- drstem-show/

Watch DrStem on The DrStem Show on Youtube for inspiration, encouragement and motivation through the interviews she conducts on the show, https://www.youtube.com/results?search_query=drstem+show

In addition to speaking and training, she counsels and coaches clients in her private practice offices in Altamonte Springs, Skype and telephonically. She serves clientele throughout the United States, Africa, the Caribbean, the United Kingdom, and Australia through one-on-one telephone coaching services.

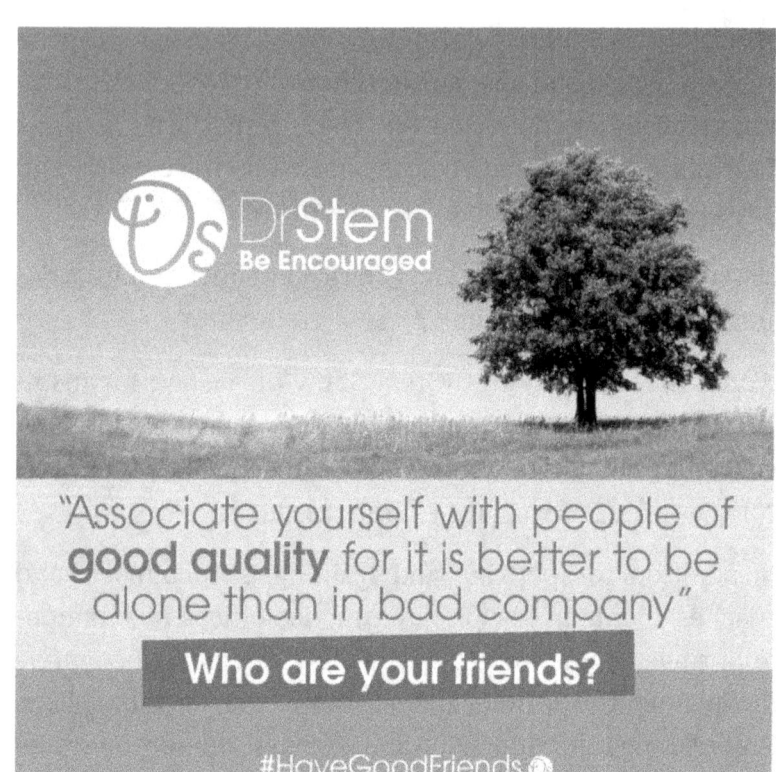

Dr. Stem is available as a trainer and speaker for on-site trainings, groups, and one- on-one coaching for parents, teenagers, women and organizations. Consultations are conducted by telephone or on-site. Her programs include:

- Bridging the Gap Between Parents and Teenagers
- Pampering The "Princess Within"
- Overcoming Being All Things to All People
- Possibilities – Turning Dreams into Reality
- Free at Last – Setting Boundaries
- How to Deal with Toxic People
- 15 Strategies to Achieve Your Dream
- How to Live a Simpler Life
- Living a New Life of Confidence- Developing A Healthy Self Esteem
- Taking Charge of Your Life, Money and Family
- Change Your Thinking – Change Your Life
- The Rollercoaster Ride Is Over! Handling Emotions
- Handling Stress: Sink, Swim or Float & More

Book Dr. Stem Mahlatini as your next motivational/inspirational speaker for your women's retreat, church, youth retreat, seminar, school assembly, or Business Management–Employee event.

Training, Individual and Group Life Coaching

Contact Dr. Stem Mahlatini at:
PHONE: (781) 254-1602

Dr. Stem authored/co-authored the following titles:

1. Beyond the Tears-Bruised but Not Broken- Author Biography-A story of Hope & Encouragement
2. The Power of Prayer & Belief
3. It's Time to Shift -From Fear to Faith
4. Finding Your True Self
5. Emotional Wellness for Women vol. 1
6. Emotional Wellness for Women vol. II
7. Emotional Wellness for Women vol. III
8. The Baby Boomer's Handbook for Women
9. The Power of God
10. Celebration of Life-Inspiration for Women
11. How to Survive When Your Ship Is Sinking: Weathering Life's Storms
12. Beyond the Scars: Real Life Accounts for Women Who Overcame Adversity
13. Confident not Corky: Why self-esteem is Key to a Successful Life, Business and Career
14. Unstoppable: A woman's Guide to Self- confidence book and workbook.

15. Zero Limits: A Teenager's Guide to Life's choices
16. 47 1/2 Things to Say to Your Teenager and How to Say Them
17. 47 1/2 Things Teenagers Need to Know About Getting Along with Their Parents
18. CDC- Courage Determination Confidence: A Teenager's Handbook to Socially Acceptable Life Skills
19. 365 Daily Success & Motivation Doses for Teens
20. 50; A celebration of Life Lessons
21. Dose of Motivation & Encouragement for Teachers
22. Profits are Better than Wages: The key to Living Your Dreams
23. Finding your True Self – Bringing Clarity and Purpose to Your Life
24. Respect- Connecting with Disconnected Students: Seven Steps to Reach the Students You Teach
25. The Blessings of Being a Woman: Embracing Womanhood
26. Build Confidence, Achieve Success
27. Success within reach: reconditioning your paradigm

Be *Original* Encouraged

You can **never make** the **same mistake twice** because the second time you make it, it's not a mistake, **it's a choice.**

DrStem

BONUS

Text Message Codes Used By Teenagers Today

If your teenage son or daughter has a smartphone, they may be using a series of secret codes to communicate with friends without you or other parents knowing what they're saying.

Most adults know at least a few of the acronyms, like "LOL" for laughing out loud, "JK" for just kidding and "LY" for love you. At least that is what I knew before working with teenagers...

If you dare to peek at their tweets and posts, you'll find a language of all their own. So here is a peek at what I know....But please do not attempt to use them as well because it's just not cool...

1. 174 ' Meet at a party spot
2. 420 ' Marijuana reference
3. 53X ' Code for sex
4. 8 ' Code for oral sex
5. 99 ' Parents are gone
6. CU46 ' See you for sex
7. 9 & CD9 ' "Code 9", parents are around
8. GNOC ' Get naked on cam
9. GYOP ' Get your pants off
10. IWSN ' I want sex now

11. KMN ' Kill me now
12. KMS ' Kill myself
13. KYS ' Kill yourself
14. LH6 ' Let's have sex
15. MOS ' Mom over shoulder
16. MPFB ' My personal **** buddy
17. Netflix and chill ' Getting together and hooking up
18. NIFOC ' Nude in front of computer
19. P911 ' Parent alert
20. PAW ' Parents are watching
21. PIR ' Parent in room
22. TDTM ' Talk dirty to me
23. Thot ' Stands for "that hoe over there" and is often used instead of "slut"
24. TWD ' Texting while driving
25. WTTP ' Want to trade pics?
26. **AF:** "I'm hungry AF."
27. **Bae:** Babe or baby, romantic
28. **Bye Felicia:** term said when you want an annoying person to buzz off.
29. **143:** I love you
30. **2DAY:** Today
31. **4EAE:** For ever and ever
32. **ADN:** Any day now
33. **AFAIK:** As far as I know

34. **AFK:** Away from keyboard
35. **ATM:** At the moment
36. **B/C:** Because
37. **B4:** Before
38. **BF / GF:** Boyfriend / Girlfriend
39. **BFN:** Bye for now
40. **BOL:** Be on later
41. **BRB:** Be right back
42. **BTW:** By the way
43. **DM:** <u>Direct message</u>
44. **DWBH:** Don't worry, be happy
45. **F2F or FTF:** Face to face
46. **FB:** Facebook
47. **FF:** Follow Friday is a recurring topic on Twitter.
48. **FTL:** For the loss / For the lose
49. **FTW:** For the win
50. **FWB** :Friends with benefits
51. **FWIW:** For what it's worth
52. **FYEO:** For your eyes only
53. **FYI:** For your information
54. **GLHF:** Good luck, have fun
55. **GR8:** Great
56. **HAK:** Hugs and kisses
57. **HAND:** Have a nice day

58. **HT or H/T:** Hat tip or heard through
59. **HTH:** Hope this helps / Happy to help
60. **IANAL:** I am not a lawyer
61. **IDK:** I don't know
62. **IIRC:** If I remember correctly
63. **IKR:** I know, right?
64. **ILY / ILU:** I love you
65. **IMHO:** In my honest opinion / In my humble opinion
66. **IMO:** In my opinion
67. **IRL:** In real life
68. **IU2U:** It's up to you
69. **IYKWIM:** If you know what I mean
70. **J/K:** Just kidding
71. **J4F:** Just for fun
72. **JIC:** Just in case
73. **JSYK:** Just so you know
74. **K or KK:** Okay
75. **LMBO:** Laughing my butt off
76. **LMK:** Let me know
77. **LOL:** Laughing out loud
78. **MM:** Music Monday.
79. **MSM:** Mainstream media
80. **NAGI:** Not a good idea
81. **NM:** Never mind

82. **NMU:** Not much, you?
83. **NP:** No problem or Now playing
84. **NSFW:** Not safe for work.
85. **NSFL:** Not safe for life.
86. **NTS:** Note to self
87. **OH:** Overheard
88. **OMG:** Oh my God
89. **ORLY:** Oh, really?
90. **PAW:** Parents are watching
91. **PLS or PLZ:** Please
92. **PPL:** People
93. **PTB:** Please text back
94. **QQ:** Crying.
95. **RAK:** Random act of kindness
96. **RL:** Real life
97. **ROFL:** Rolling on the floor laughing
98. **RT:** Retweet.
99. **RUOK:** Are you okay?
100. **SMH:** Shaking my head
101. **SRSLY:** Seriously
102. **SSDD:** Same stuff, different day
103. **SWAK:** Sealed with a kiss
104. **SWYP:** So, what's your problem?
105. **TIA:** Thanks in advance
106. **TIME:** Tears in my eyes

107. **TMB:** Tweet me back
108. **TMI:** Too much information
109. **TMRW:** Tomorrow
110. **TTYL:** Talk to you later
111. **TY or TU:** Thank you
112. **VSF:** Very sad face
113. **WB:** Welcome back
114. **WTH:** What the heck?
115. **WTPA:** Where the party at?
116. **WYCM:** Will you call me?
117. **YGM:** You've got
118. **YMMV:** Your mileage may vary
119. **YW:** You're welcome
120. **ZOMG:** Oh my god (sarcastic)

www.ingramcontent.com/pod-product-compliance
Lightning Source LLC
Chambersburg PA
CBHW052055070526
44584CB00017B/2191